THE GERMAN CAMPAIGNS IN THE BALKANS (SPRING 1941)

FOREWORD

The purpose of this study is to describe the German campaigns in the Balkans and the seizure of Crete within the framework of Hitler's military policy during the second year of World War II. The study is the first of a series dealing with large-scale German military operations in Eastern Europe; other historical studies such as Germany and Finland—Allies and Enemies in World War II, The Axis Campaign in Russia, 1941–45: A Strategic Survey, and German Army Group Operations in Russia will follow.

"The German Campaigns in the Balkans" is written from the German point of view and is based mainly on original German records and postwar military writings by Dr. Helmut Greiner, General Burkhart H. Mueller-Hillebrand, and the late General Hans von Greiffenberg. The lessons and conclusions following each narrative have been drawn from the same German sources. (These records and manuscripts are listed in appendix III.) Material taken from U.S. and Allied sources has been integrated into the text, but specific cross references have been made only in those instances where these sources deviate from the German documents.

The work of preparing this study in English, which consisted of translating basic German records and manuscripts, performing additional research, expanding and then rewriting the narratives with an eye for continuity and factual data, was done chiefly by Mr. George E. Blau of the Foreign Studies Branch, Special Studies Division, Office of the Chief of Military History. In the process of presenting the material, every effort has been made to give a balanced account of German strategy and operations in the Balkans during the spring of 1941.

A. C. SMITH
Major General, USA
Chief, Military History

CONTENTS

PART ONE. THE MILITARY-POLITICAL SITUATION IN THE BALKANS *Page*
(October 1940–March 1941) 1

Chapter 1. The Great Powers
 I. Germany 2
 II. Italy 3
 III. Soviet Union 7
 IV. Great Britain 9

Chapter 2. Germany's Satellites in the Balkans
 I. Hungary 10
 II. Romania 10
 III. Bulgaria 12

Chapter 3. The Other Balkan Countries
 I. Turkey 16
 II. Yugoslavia 20

PART TWO. THE YUGOSLAV CAMPAIGN (Operation 25)

Chapter 4. Political and Strategic Planning 25
 I. Military Topography 26
 II. Hitler's Concept of the Strategic Factors 27

Chapter 5. The Plan of Attack
 I. The Outline Plan 29
 II. The Timing of the Attacks 30
 III. Second Army 31
 IV. First Panzer Group 32
 V. XLI Panzer Corps 33

Chapter 6. The Defense Forces
 I. General 33
 II. Defensive Plans 33
 III. Training and Tactics 35
 IV. Guerrilla Warfare 35
 V. Fortifications 36
 VI. Order of Battle 36
 VII. Deficiencies and Confusion 37

Chapter 7. The Attack Forces
 I. Command Posts 38
 II. The Luftwaffe 39
 III. Second Army 39
 IV. First Panzer Group 41
 V. XLI Panzer Corps 41

		Page
Chapter 8. Logistical Planning and Assembly of Second Army		
	I. The Rail Transportation Problem	42
	II. The Danube as a Route of Transportation	44
	III. Other Logistical Planning	46
	IV. The Assembly of Second Army	47
Chapter 9. Operations		
	I. The Air Bombardment of Belgrade	49
	II. The Three-Pronged Drive on the Yugoslav Capital	50
	III. Secondary Attacks	55
	IV. Italian and Hungarian Operations	60
	V. The Final Drive on Sarajevo	61
	VI. Armistice Negotiations	63
	VII. Losses	64
Chapter 10. Lessons		
	I. General	64
	II. Coalition Warfare	65
	III. Assembly	65
	IV. Other Organizational and Tactical Improvisations	66
Chapter 11. Conclusions		
	I. Yugoslav Military Unpreparedness	66
	II. Internal Disunity	68
	III. German Propaganda	69
	IV. Seeds of Unrest	69

PART THREE. THE GERMAN CAMPAIGN IN GREECE (Operation MARITA)

Chapter 12. General		
	I. Political and Military Events (October 1940–April 1941)	70
	II. Military Topography	74
	III. Strategic Factors	77
Chapter 13. The Defense Forces		
	I. Yugoslav Forces	79
	II. Greek Forces	79
	III. British and Imperial Forces	80
Chapter 14. The Attack Forces		81
15. The Plan of Attack		82
16. The Assembly—Logistical Problems		83
17. Operations		
	I. The German Thrust across Southern Yugoslavia	86
	II. The 2d Panzer Division Drive to Salonika	87
	III. The Struggle across the Metaxas Line	88
	IV. The Seizure of Western Thrace	89
	V. Capitulation of the Greek Second Army	89
	VI. The German Estimate of the Situation on 9 April	89
	VII. The Breakthrough to Kozani	91
	VIII. The Withdrawal of the Greek First Army	94

Chapter 17. Operations—Continued

		Page
IX.	Securing the German Rear Areas	96
X.	The Fighting near Mount Olympus	96
XI.	Continuation of the XL Panzer Corps Drive	100
XII.	Regrouping of German Forces	102
XIII.	The Last British Stand at Thermopylae	104
XIV.	The Seizure of the Isthmus of Corinth	107
XV.	The German Drive on Athens and across the Peloponnesus	111
XVI.	Losses	112

Chapter 18. Lessons

I.	Employment of Armor in Mountainous Terrain	112
II.	Air Support	112
III.	Flying Columns	112
IV.	Mission-Type Orders	114
V.	Mountain Training and Equipment	114
VI.	Patrol Activities	114
VII.	Obstacles and Demolitions	116
VIII.	Pacification of Enemy Territory	116

Chapter 19. Conclusions 116

PART FOUR. THE SEIZURE OF CRETE (Operation MERKUR)

Chapter 20. General

I.	Strategic Factors and Planning	119
II.	Situation in the Eastern Mediterranean	120
III.	Military Topography	121
IV.	The Defense Forces	123
V.	The Attack Forces	124
VI.	The Plan of Attack	126
VII.	The Assembly—Logistical Problems	127

Chapter 21. Operations

I.	The Initial Airborne Landings (20 May 1941)	129
II.	The Seaborne Invasion (20–22 May)	133
III.	The Continuation of the Struggle (21 May–1 June)	133
VI.	Casualties and Losses	140

Chapter 22. Lessons 141

23. Conclusions 147

PART FIVE. THE RELATIONSHIP BETWEEN THE CAMPAIGNS IN THE BALKANS AND THE INVASION OF RUSSIA 148

Chapter 24. Influence of the Plans for Operation BARBAROSSA on the Campaigns in the Balkans

I.	Hasty Execution of the Balkan Campaigns	149
II.	Hurried Redeployment from the Balkans	149
III.	Defective Occupation of Yugoslavia and Greece	149

Chapter 25. Effect of the Balkan Campaigns on Operation BARBAROSSA *Page*

    I. Delay of Operation BARBAROSSA 150
    II. The Redeployment of the Ground Forces 150
    III. The Influence on Air Operations 151
    IV. The Balkan Campaigns as a Diversion 151

Chapter 26. Conclusions 152

APPENDICES

    I. German Chain of Command at the Start of the Balkan Campaigns (6 April 1941) 152
    II. Chronological Table of Events 153
    III. Bibliographic List 158

MAPS
No.
1. General Reference Map 1
2. German Operations and Plans—July 1940–March 1941 5
3. The Campaigns in the Balkans—Deployment and Initial Objectives ... 42
4. The German Campaign in Yugoslavia (Operation 25) 49
5. The German Campaign in Greece (Operation MARITA) 70
6. The Strategic Importance of Crete 119
7. The Seizure of Crete (Operation MERKUR) 122

ILLUSTRATIONS
No.
1. The Military Bridge across the Danube 18
2. Bridge across the Drava River Damaged by the Yugoslavs 28
3. Yugoslav Obstacles across the Railway Tracks near Spielfeld 34
4. German Supply Column Crossing a 4,100-Foot Pass in Bulgaria 40
5. German Emergency Bridge Replaces Demolished Structure 45
6. Prime Movers Towing Heavy Trucks along Muddy Road 51
7. German Patrol Returning from a Raid across the Yugoslav Border ... 56
8. Man and Beast Working Together to Pull Vehicles out of the Mud ... 59
9. German Mark III Tank Advancing through Mountain Pass Protected by Flak 62
10. Disabled Yugoslav Tank 67
11. Gun Emplacements in a Greek Mountain Position 73
12. Antitank Obstacles along the Metaxas Line 76
13. Obstacles along the Yugoslav-Greek Border 78
14. German Infantry Marching through Bulgarian Mountains toward the Greek Border 80
15. Oxen and Horses Hitched in Tandem to German Field Kitchen in the Mountains of Bulgaria 85
16. German Artillery Firing at Metaxas Line Fortifications 87
17. Metaxas Line Defenses near Rupel Gorge 88
18. Road Block near Greek Border 90
19. Mountain Division on the March through Northern Greece 92
20. German Infantry "Invading" Islands in the Agean Sea 95
21. German Tank Burns during Attack on the Ridge near Platamon ... 97
22. German Tank Descending Slope toward Pinios River 99
23. German Tanks Get Stuck during the Crossing of the Pinios River .. 101

No.		Page
24.	German Convoy Waiting to Cross the Pinios River on a Pneumatic Boat Ferry	103
25.	German Tanks Approaching the Thermopylae Pass	105
26.	Construction of an Emergency Bridge near Thermopylae Pass	106
27.	The Airborne Operation against the Isthmus of Corinth	108
28.	Right: The Destruction of the Corinth Canal Bridge. Top: The Canal after the Explosion	109
29.	Motorized Column Advancing along the Railroad Tracks from Thebes to Athens	110
30.	A Motorized and a Mountain Infantry Column Share Road to Athens	113
31.	Difficult Terrain in Central Greece	115
32.	German Engineer Using Mine Detector	117
33.	German Motor Sailer Three Miles Southwest of Cape Spatha	125
34.	Mountain Troops Preparing for Airlift to Crete	128
35.	Maleme Airfield with Hill 107 in Background	131
36.	Airborne Landings West of Maleme	134
37.	Disabled British Tank near Canea	136
38.	The Struggle for Heraklion Airfield	138
39.	The First Mules Have Arrived in Crete	140
40.	Airborne Landings over the North Coast of Crete	144
41.	Antitank Gun, Attached to Five Parachutes, Is Dropped over Crete	146

(Most of the illustrations are U. S. Army photos from captured German films; a few are reproductions from the collection of captured combat paintings now in the custody of the Chief of Military History, Special Staff, U. S. Army.)

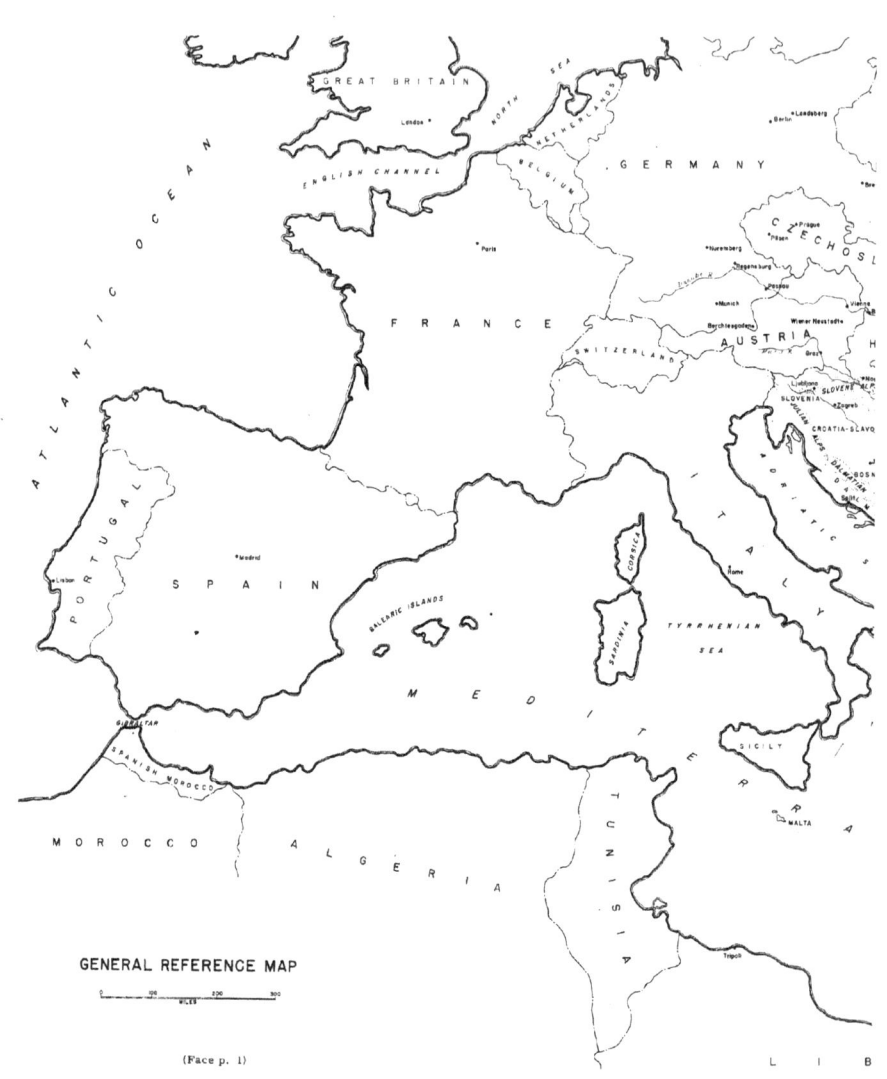

GENERAL REFERENCE MAP

(Face p. 1)

PART ONE
THE MILITARY-POLITICAL SITUATION IN THE BALKANS
(October 1940–March 1941)

During the latter half of 1940 the Balkans, always a notorious hotbed of intrigues, became the center of conflicting interests of Germany, Italy, Russia, and Great Britain. From the beginning of World War II Adolf Hitler had consistently stated that Germany had no territorial ambitions in the Balkans. Because his primary interest in that area was of an economic nature—Germany obtained vital oil and food supplies from the Balkan countries—he was prepared to do his utmost to preserve peace in that part of Europe. For this reason he attempted to keep in check Italy's aggressive Balkan policy, to satisfy Hungarian and Bulgarian claims to Romanian territory by peaceful means, and to avoid any incident which might lead to Great Britain's direct intervention in Greece. It was no easy task to synchronize so many divergent political actions at a time when Germany was preparing the invasion of the British Isles and later planning as alternate measures the capture of Gibraltar, the occupation of Egypt and the Suez Canal, and the attack on Russia.

The unprecedented speed with which Germany had conquered western Europe in 1940 had immediate repercussions in the Balkan countries, some of which had previously belonged to the French sphere of influence. By applying diplomatic pressure and undermining their internal structure Hitler led one Balkan state after another to adhere to the Tripartite Pact, which had been signed by Germany, Italy, and Japan on 27 September 1940 (see app. II, Chronological Table of Events). In general, shortly after a new member had signed the pact, a German military mission would cross its border and gradually assume control over communications, airfields, and internal security.

For a better understanding of the military operations that took place in the Balkans during the spring of 1941, it is necessary to analyze the political events that led to the outbreak of hostilities.

This publication replaces DA Pam 20–260, November 1953.

Chapter 1

The Great Powers

I. Germany

After the signing of the Franco-German armistice on 21 June 1940, Hitler believed that Great Britain would be prepared to come to an understanding since British forces had been driven off the Continent and France had been subdued. However, soon after his return to Berlin on 6 July it became evident that the British Government, far from entertaining any ideas of reconciliation, was determined to carry on the war. German preparations for the invasion of Great Britain were pushed with vigor. Hitler's speculations as to the reasons for Great Britain's stubborn refusal to come to terms led him, as early as 21 July 1940, to the belief that Prime Minister Winston S. Churchill hoped for Russia's entry into the war against Germany. On 31 July Hitler mentioned for the first time since the conclusion of the Russo-German treaty that he would be forced to invade Russia and that the attack would have to be launched in the spring of 1941. He requested the Army General Staff to study the various aspects of a campaign against Russia and directed that, in its organizational planning for the future, the Army must not lose sight of the possibility of a war with the Soviet Union. This request was subsequently repeated during the discussion of other plans.

Taking cognizance of the failure of the air offensive against the British Isles, Hitler decided on 12 October 1940 that the invasion of England would have to be postponed until the following year. Since the plans for a direct invasion were thus shelved, another way had to be found to defeat Great Britain without venturing a cross-Channel attack. Alternative operations in the Mediterranean had been under consideration as early as the end of July, and now Hitler ordered the Army to draw up plans for the capture of Gibraltar on the assumption that Spain would permit the passage of German troops through its territory. Moreover, Italy planned to invade Egypt at the beginning of August 1940 by launching a series of offensive actions from its Libyan bases. In Hitler's opinion, the Italians would not be able to stage the final decisive drive into the Nile delta before the autumn of 1941. German forces were to participate in the final phase of the operation, and the Army High Command was instructed to prepare the necessary forces—approximately one panzer corps—for desert warfare in a tropical climate. Since the Germans lacked experience in this type of warfare, appropriate motor transportation, equipment, ammunition, and clothing had to be developed and produced.

While Germany was preparing to intervene at both ends of the Mediterranean, peace in the Balkans had to be maintained at any cost. Hitler believed that this could best be achieved by forcing Romania to cede the territories claimed by Hungary and Bulgaria and by lining up the Balkan countries on the Axis side.

The dismemberment of Romania was accomplished in successive stages. Russian occupation of Bessarabia and northern Bukovina at the end of June 1940 gave added impetus to Hungarian and Bulgarian revisionist claims. The Romanian Government therefore issued orders for general mobilization to defend its territory. Germany and Italy had to use all their influence to prevent an armed conflict. Hitler's intervention in favor of Bulgaria led to the cession of the southern Dobrudja by Romania on 21 August 1940. By then only the Hungarian claims remained to be settled. This was achieved by the Vienna Arbitration Award, which took place on 30 August. Romania was forced to yield to Hungary one third of Transylvania, that is, some 16,600 square miles with a population of 2.4 million inhabitants. Even more important than the partition of Transylvania, however, was the Axis Powers' guarantee to defend the territorial integrity of what was left of Romania. This guarantee was clearly directed against the Soviet Union. In Romania the various territorial concessions caused a political overturn, bringing General Ion Antonescu to power. Upon the general's request the first elements of the German military mission entered Romania on 7 October. German Army and Luftwaffe units were to protect the oil fields, train and reorganize the Romanian military forces, and prepare the ground for a possible attack on Russia from Romanian bases.

II. Italy

Neither the Italian nor the Soviet Government received official notification of the entry of German troops into Romania. This was all the more surprising to Mussolini because Italy and Germany had given a joint guarantee to Romania. He was very indignant about being faced with a *fait accompli* and decided to pay Hitler back in his own coin by attempting to seize Greece without giving official notice to Germany. Mussolini expected that the occupation of Greece would be a mere police action, similar to Germany's seizure of Czechoslovakia in the spring of 1939. On two preceding occasions Hitler had agreed that the Mediterranean and Adriatic were exclusively Italian spheres of interest. Since Yugoslavia and Greece were situated within these spheres, Mussolini felt entitled to adopt whatever policy he saw fit. There was no reason why the man who had revived the *Mare Nostrum* concept should hesitate to demonstrate to the entire world that his twentieth century Romans were as superior to their Mediterranean rivals as their ancestors had been to the Greeks 2,000 years ago.

In Mussolini's opinion one of the main attractions of an attack on Greece was that Italy would not have to depend on Germany's assistance for the execution of such an operation. On 15 October he decided to invade Greece, although he knew that the Germans would disapprove. The attack was launched on 28 October, and the almost immediate setbacks of the Italians only served to heighten Hitler's displeasure. What enraged the Fuehrer most was that his repeated statements of the need for peace in the Balkans had been ignored by Mussolini.

The German military experts also disapproved the Italian plan of operations, but for other reasons. In their opinion any campaign in the Balkans would have to be executed in a manner similar to the one applied by the Germans in the campaign in Norway. The strategically important features would have to be seized in blitzkrieg fashion. In the Balkans these points were not situated along the Albanian border but in southern Greece and on Crete. The Italian failure to capture Crete seemed a strategic blunder, since British possession of the island endangered the Italian lines of communication to North Africa and assured Greece of a steady flow of supplies from Egypt. Moreover, the British bombers were now within range of the Romanian oil fields that the Germans had secured at such great effort.

Hitler's decision to intervene in the military operations in the Balkans was made on 4 November, seven days after Italy had attacked Greece through Albania and four days after the British had occupied Crete and Limnos. He ordered the Army General Staff to prepare plans for the invasion of northern Greece from Romania via Bulgaria. The operation was to deprive the British of bases for future ground and air operations across the restive Balkans against the Romanian oil fields. Moreover, it would indirectly assist the Italians by diverting Greek forces from Albania.

The plans for this campaign, together with the projects involving Gibraltar and North Africa, were incorporated into a master plan to deprive the British of all their Mediterranean bases. On 12 November 1940 the Armed Forces High Command issued Directive No. 18, in which Hitler outlined his plan for the conduct of future operations to the three services. He first mentioned that Vichy France was to

GERMAN OPERATIONS AND PLANS
July 1940 - March 1941

(Face p. 5)

Map 2

LEGEND:

⟿ Territory under German military control at the end of June 1940

▶ Operations carried out

▬▬▶ Operations not carried out

(1) INVASION OF GREAT BRITAIN:
    First discussion of the plan ———————Toward the end of June 1940
    Order to start preparations. ————————16 July 1940
    Intended start of the operation:——————September 1940
    Cancellation of the operations order:————12 October 1940

(2) INCREASED AIR AND NAVAL WARFARE AGAINST ENGLAND:
    First discussion of the plan.————————July 1940
    Order to start preparations:——————————1 August 1940
    Start of the operations:——————————8 August 1940

(3) GIBRALTAR: First discussion of the plan:—————————September 1940
    Order to start preparations. ——————————12 November 1940
    Intended start of the operation:————————January 1941
    Cancellation of the operations order:————8 December 1940

(4) SEIZURE OF UNOCCUPIED FRANCE:
    Order to start preparations. ————————10 December 1940
    Execution of the operation. ————————November 1942

(5) PARTICIPATION IN ITALIAN OFFENSIVE TOWARD EGYPT (SUEZ CANAL)
    Order to start preparations.—————————12 November 1940
    Intended start of the operation——————Autumn 1941
    (Actually, operations in support of the Italians started already at an earlier moment, but with defensive objectives)

(6) OPERATION MARITA:
    First discussion of the plan ———————4 November 1940
    Order to start preparations:—————————13 December 1940
    Start of the operation:————————————6 April 1941

(7) OPERATION 25:
    First discussion & order to start preparations:—————27 March 1941
    Start of the operation:——————————6 April 1941

(8) OPERATION BARBAROSSA
    First discussion of the plan:————————End of July 1940
    Order to start preparations ————————18 December 1940
    Intended start of the operation:——————15 May 1941
    Start of the operation:——————————22 June 1941

be given an opportunity for defending its African possessions against the British and Free French. Gibraltar was to be seized and the straits closed, while at the same time the British were to be prevented from landing elsewhere on the Iberian Peninsula. German forces were to support the Italians in their offensive against Egypt, if and when the latter reached Mersa Matruh. The Luftwaffe, in particular, was to make preparations for attacking Alexandria and the Suez Canal. The Army was to ready ten divisions for the seizure of northern Greece, possession of which would permit German flying formations to operate against British air bases in the eastern Mediterranean and thus protect the Romanian oil fields. (Map 2)

The operations against Gibraltar and Greece were scheduled to take place simultaneously in January 1941, while the German offensive in North Africa was to be launched in the autumn of that year. The invasion of the British Isles was also mentioned in this directive, the target date of which was tentatively scheduled for the spring of 1941. The particular difficulty involved in the execution of some of these plans was that the German Army was supposed to conduct operations across the seas even though the Axis had not gained naval superiority in the respective areas. On 4 November even Hitler had voiced doubts as to the advisability of conducting offensive operations in North Africa, since Italy did not control the Mediterranean. That these doubts were well founded became apparent when, on 6 November, British naval air forces inflicted a severe defeat on the Italian Navy at Taranto.

The German displeasure at the ill-timed Italian attack on Greece found its expression in a letter Hitler addressed to Mussolini on 20 November 1940. Among other things, he stated:

> I wanted, above all, to ask you to postpone the operation until a more favorable season, in any case until after the presidential election in America. In any event I wanted to ask you not to undertake this action without previously carrying out a blitzkrieg operation on Crete. For this purpose I intended to make practical suggestions regarding the employment of a parachute and of an airborne division.

After enumerating the psychological and military consequences of the Italian failure in Albania, the Fuehrer suggested a number of countermeasures to restore the situation. Spain would have to be induced to enter the war as soon as possible in order to deny the British the use of Gibraltar and to block the western entrance to the Mediterranean. Every possible means would have to be employed to divert Russia's interest from the Balkans to the Near East. Special efforts would have to be made to arrive at an agreement with Turkey whereby Turkish pressure on Bulgaria would be relieved. Yugoslavia would have to be induced to adopt a neutral attitude or, if possible, be led to collaborate actively with the Axis in solving the Greek problem. In the Balkans any military operation that was to lead to a success could be risked only after Yugoslavia's position had been fully clarified. Hungary would have to grant permission for the immediate transit of sizable German units destined for Romania. The latter country would have to accept the reinforcement of the German troops guaranteeing the protection of its territory. Hitler then continued by stating that he had decided to prevent any British buildup in northeastern Greece by force, whatever the risk may be.

In his reply of 22 November Mussolini expressed his regrets about the misunderstandings with regard to Greece. The Italian forces had been halted because of bad weather, the desertion of nearly all the Albanian forces incorporated into Italian units, and Bulgaria's attitude, which permitted the Greeks to shift eight divisions from Thrace to Albania.

In December 1940 the German plans in the Mediterranean underwent considerable change when, at the beginning of the month, Franco rejected the plan for an attack on Gibraltar. Consequently, German offensive planning for southern Europe had to be restricted to the campaign against Greece. Upon insistence of the Luftwaffe, the entire country was to be occupied, not just the northern provinces. For this purpose the Armed Forces High Command issued Directive No. 20, dated 13 December 1940, which outlined the Greek campaign under the code designation, Operation **MARITA**. In the introductory part of the directive Hitler pointed out that, in view of the confused situation in Albania, it was particularly important to thwart British attempts to establish air bases in Greece, which would constitute a threat to Italy as well as to the Romanian oil fields. To meet this situation twenty-four German divisions were to be assembled gradually in southern Romania within the next few months, ready to enter Bulgaria as soon as they received orders. In March, when the weather would be more favorable, they were to occupy the northern coast of the Aegean Sea and, if necessary, the entire Greek mainland. Bulgaria's assistance was expected; support by Italian forces and the coordination of the German and Italian operations in the Balkans would be the subject of future discussions. The Luftwaffe was to provide air protection during the assembly period and prepare bases in Romania. During the operation the Luftwaffe was to neutralize the enemy air force, support the ground forces, and whenever possible capture British bases on Greek islands by executing airborne landings.

Meanwhile, the Luftwaffe was to assist the Italians in stabilizing the precarious situation on the Albanian front. This was to be accomplished by airlifting approximately 30,000 Italian troops and great quantities of equipment and supplies from the Italian mainland to Albania.

Even though Hitler had decided to attack Greece, he wanted to tread softly in the Balkans so as not to expand the conflict during the winter. If Turkey entered the war against Germany, the chances for a successful invasion of Russia would diminish because of the diversion of forces such a new conflict would involve. Moreover, at the beginning of December 1940 the British launched an offensive from Egypt and drove the Italians back to the west. Toward the end of the month the situation of the Italians in Libya grew more and more critical. By January 1941 their forces in North Africa were in danger of being completely annihilated. If that happened, Italy with its indefensible coast line would be exposed to an enemy invasion. To forestall such disastrous developments, German air units under the command of X Air Corps had previously been transferred to Sicily, and the movement of German Army elements to Tripoli via Italy was begun immediately. In February initial small contingents of German ground troops arrived in North Africa, and the critical situation was soon alleviated. The first German troops to arrive were elements of a panzer division under the command of General Erwin Rommel. Hitler ordered these forces to protect Tripoli by a series of limited-objective attacks, thus relieving the pressure on the Italian troops. The political objective of this military intervention was to prevent Italy's internal collapse which would almost certainly result from the loss of her African possessions.

III. Soviet Union

Following the conclusion of the Russo-German alliance in August 1939, Hitler's policy was to try to divert Russian expansionist ambitions. He wanted to interest the Soviet rulers in a southeastward drive to the Persian Gulf and the Arabian Sea. However, there were many indications that the Russians were more interested in the Dardanelles and the Danube delta, where their political and military aspirations clashed with German economic interests. When the Russians showed their bad faith by subjugating the Baltic States and forcing Romania to relinquish Bessarabia and northern Bukovina while Germany was preoccupied with the campaign in the West, Hitler felt that the Soviet Union would surely take advantage of the diversion of strong German forces into distant Mediterranean areas by exerting political pressure on some of the Balkan countries.

Hitler's apprehensions were all the more justified because the Soviet Union intensified its political activities in the Balkans, particularly in Bulgaria, as soon as the Russian troops had established themselves at the mouth of the Danube, Germany's principal supply line from the east. By the autumn of 1940 Russo-German relations had further deteriorated considerably as the result of the Vienna Award, the presence of the German military mission in Romania, and Soviet pressure on Bulgaria.

These problems, as well as the entire question of the future relationship between Germany and the Soviet Union, were to be the subject of discussions between Molotov and the German political leaders during the former's visit to Berlin on 12–13 November 1940. All areas of disagreement were to be covered during these discussions and, if possible, the foundations for a common policy were to be laid at the same time. It is interesting to note that German planning for the invasion of the USSR was already well advanced. A tentative plan for the Russian campaign had been submitted on 5 August and Directive No. 21 for Operation BARBAROSSA, which was issued on 18 December, was being drafted by the Army General Staff. Directive No. 18, issued on the day of Molotov's arrival in the German capital, stipulated that preparations for Operation BARBAROSSA were to be continued regardless of the outcome of the conversations.

During his conversations with Hitler, Molotov stated that, as a Black Sea power, the Soviet Union was interested in a number of Balkan countries. He asked Hitler whether the German-Italian guarantee to Romania could not be revoked because, in his opinion, it was directed against the Soviet Union. Hitler refused to give way on this question and did not commit himself on the subject of a Russian guarantee for Bulgaria, by which Molotov intended to reestablish the balance of power in the Balkans. Nor was Hitler prepared to help the Soviet Union to arrive at an agreement with Turkey regarding the settlement of the Dardanelles question. As to Greece, the Fuehrer intimated that Germany would take all military steps necessary to prevent Great Britain from establishing itself in that country. The conference ended in a deadlock.

IV. Great Britain

During the spring of 1940 Hitler was greatly concerned over the possibility of British intervention in the Balkans. Had not Britain and France tried to establish a solid political and military front in the Balkans by concluding a series of agreements with Turkey, by trying to draw Yugoslavia into their orbit, and by consolidating their position in the Aegean? Germany's first countermeasures came in May and June 1940, when Romania was induced to repudiate the Anglo-French territorial guarantee after it had been pressured into signing a pact which stipulated that the Romanians would step up their oil production and would make maximum deliveries to the Axis Powers. British personnel supervising the operation of the oil fields were dismissed during the month of July. After the Vienna Award of August 1940, Romania intended to break off diplomatic relations with Britain, but after consultation with Berlin this action was postponed because of the potential danger of British air attacks on the oil fields.

When Greece was attacked by Italy on 28 October 1940, it did not request any assistance from Great Britain, for fear of giving Hitler an excuse for German intervention. Nevertheless, the British occupied Crete and Limnos three days later, thereby improving their strategic position in the eastern Mediterranean. By 4 November British air force units began to arrive in southern Greece. Since Hitler believed that these moves brought the Romanian oil fields within British bombing range, he decided to transfer additional antiaircraft, fighter, and fighter-bomber units to Romania to protect the German oil resources.

When the German threat began to take more definite shape during the winter of 1940-41, the Greek Government decided to accept the British offer to send air force units to northern Greece to strengthen the defense of Salonika. Early in March 1941, the British sent an expeditionary corps of some 53,000 troops into Greece in an attempt to support their allies against the impending German invasion.

However, before Germany could think of starting military operations in the Balkans, it had to secure its lines of communication. For this purpose it had to obtain firm political control over Hungary, Romania, and Bulgaria, and to wrest some important concessions and assurances from Turkey and Yugoslavia.

Chapter 2
Germany's Satellites in the Balkans

I. Hungary

The strong German forces needed for the attack on Greece could be assembled in Romania only after the Hungarian Government had granted them free passage through that country. The first step in that direction was to obtain Hungary's adherence to the Tripartite Pact. On 20 November Hungarian Premier Teleki signed the pact in Berchtesgaden, and Hitler mentioned on that occasion that he intended to assist the Italians in Greece, thus preparing the way for later demands he intended to make on Hungary.

II. Romania

During the second part of October 1940 General Antonescu made urgent requests to speed up the reinforcement of the German military mission in Romania. According to his indications there was a grave danger of a Russian attack on Romania. By mid-November the 13th Motorized Infantry Division, reinforced by the 4th Panzer Regiment, engineer, and signal troops, six fighter and two reconnaissance squadrons, and some antiaircraft units had arrived in Romania. On the occasion of Romania's adherence to the Tripartite Pact, which took place on 23 November, Hitler informed Antonescu of his plans against Greece. Romania would not be required to lend active assistance in the attack on Greece, but was to permit the assembly of German forces in its territory.

Antonescu's conference with Field Marshal Wilhelm Keitel, the chief of OKW (Armed Forces High Command), which took place on 24 November, was of great importance to Romania's future. Romania's plans called for the organization of thirty-nine divisions. Motorization was the principal bottleneck but, because of Germany's shortage of rubber, Keitel could not offer Antonescu any tires. The Romanian chief of state then explained his country's plan of defense against an attack by the Soviet Union. Keitel reassured him that the German Army would lend immediate assistance to the Romanian forces in the event of a Russian invasion which, however, he considered unlikely. As a result of this conversation the German military mission was reinforced by the transfer of the 16th Panzer Division to Romania during the second half of December.

Meanwhile, the German Army General Staff had initiated the preparations for Operations MARITA and BARBAROSSA and had drawn up the schedule for the concentration of forces and the plan of operation. On 5 December these plans were submitted to Hitler with the observation that it would not be possible to start MARITA before the snow had melted at the beginning of March. The completed plan would have to be drawn up by the middle of December since the assembly would require seventy-eight days. No definite estimate of the duration of the campaign could be given, but it would be safe to assume that it would last three to four weeks. Since the redeployment of troops would require four additional weeks and their rehabilitation would add a further delay, the units participating in the Balkan campaign would not be available for Operation BARBAROSSA before mid-May 1941.

Hitler believed that the threat of German retaliation had so far prevented the British from launching air attacks on the Romanian oil fields from Greek territory and that probably no attacks would take place during the next months. Nevertheless, Germany would have to settle the Greek problem once and for all, unless Greece took the initiative to end the conflict with Italy and force the British to withdraw from its territory. In that event, German intervention would prove unnecessary since the issue of European hegemony would not be decided in Greece. Since the Greeks had shown no intention of taking any such initiative, the assembly of forces and preparations for Operation MARITA had to be pushed energetically so that the offensive could be launched by the beginning of March 1941.

In the meantime, late in December, the first attack echelon of Twelfth Army, the headquarters that was to be in charge of the ground forces during Operation MARITA, began to entrain for Romania. The heavy bridge equipment needed for crossing the Danube was shipped on the very first trains so that it could be unloaded at the Danube wharfs by 3 January. The engineer units needed for the bridging operation had been transported to Romania during the second half of December, together with the 16th Panzer Division. They were to prepare the construction of bridges along the Danube as soon as the equipment arrived. Heavy snowfall disrupted the rail movement, and snowdrifts caused additional delays during January. Internal uprisings, which took place in Bucharest and other Romanian cities during the second half of January, were quickly suppressed by General Antonescu and therefore did not interfere with German preparations. By the end of January the Twelfth Army and First Panzer Group (a headquarters in charge of an armored force of army size, but operating in conjunction with an army) Headquarters, three corps headquarters with corps and GHQ troops, and two panzer and two infantry divisions had arrived in Romania in full strength. In conformity with Bulgaria's request, the two panzer divisions were stationed in and around Cernavoda in northern Dobrudja, while the two infantry divisions were assembled in the Craiova-Giurgiu area in southern Romania.

III. Bulgaria

A few days after Molotov's departure, on 18 November, King Boris of Bulgaria arrived in Germany. Hitler tried to persuade him to join the Tripartite Pact and discussed with him the question of Bulgarian participation in the attack on Greece. With obvious reserve, the king merely called attention to the fact that the weather and road conditions in the Greek-Bulgarian border region would not allow the commitment of major forces before the beginning of March. Moreover, he emphasized very strongly that it was of utmost importance for Bulgaria not to be openly involved in any German preparations until the last moment before the actual attack. Since Bulgaria's participation therefore appeared doubtful, Hitler decided that the number of German divisions would have to be increased.

In view of the appearance of British troops in Greece, the establishment of a German warning net in Bulgaria was of vital importance. The Bulgarian Government agreed to admit to its territory one Luftwaffe signal company consisting of 200 men, dressed in civilian clothes, who were to operate an aircraft reporting and warning service. The Luftwaffe, however, first asked permission to dispatch two companies, then a few days later increased this figure to three companies, because incoming reports indicated that the British were constructing air bases on the Greek mainland and the Aegean Islands and were bringing in a steadily increasing number of long-range bombers. The German negotiations with the Bulgarian military authorities made little progress because of the adverse effect of the reverses suffered by the Italians in Albania. By the end of 1940, however, an agreement was reached, and by mid-January all three Luftwaffe signal companies, their personnel disguised in civilian clothes, were operating on the mountain range which extends across Bulgaria.

During the political and military negotiations between German and Bulgarian leaders, the latter were very hesitant. Their attitude was motivated by fear of Turkish intervention in the event of a German attack on Greece and by concern over Soviet reaction. After the German military mission had established itself in Romania, the Soviet Union offered to send a military mission to Bulgaria. This offer, made in late November, was rejected, and the Bulgarian Government feared that, as soon as the German military intervention in Bulgaria became manifest, the Soviet Union might seek to recoup itself through the occupation of the Bulgarian Black Sea port of Varna. The Bulgarians therefore insisted that all preparatory measures that the Germans intended to take in Bulgaria be carried out in the utmost secrecy and requested that Germany supply Bulgaria with arms and equipment to reinforce the Black Sea coast defenses. This would include the delivery of modern coast artillery and antiaircraft batteries with the necessary ammunition, as well as furnishing mines and mine-laying vessels. Moreover, German naval experts were to assist in the construction of new coastal defenses.

Hitler promised early compliance with these requests in order to obtain in return some concessions from the Bulgarian Government. One concession was the permission to send a joint military mission, composed of officers from all three services who were to travel through Bulgaria disguised as civilians. Upon returning to Germany, the chief of the mission reported that, in view of the inadequate billeting facilities, the poor condition of roads and bridges, the limited supply of rations, fodder, combustibles, and motor fuel, as well as the absence of reliable maps, operations launched in the Balkans during the wet and cold seasons presented problems that were difficult, though not insurmountable. If appropriate measures, such as improving the roads, reinforcing the bridges, equipping the troops with light motor vehicles and snowplows, employing more German transportation experts, and preparing better maps, were introduced, the attack could be launched even in winter. Since it was generally assumed that major military operations in the Balkans were not practicable in winter, it would be all the easier to camouflage Operation **MARITA**, inasmuch as nobody would believe that the Germans were feverishly planning and preparing an operation for that time of the year. As an initial step, Bulgaria should permit the entry of a mission of technical experts, whose presence would be kept secret. The mission was to supervise the improvement of the road net and bridges by indigenous labor forces and get acquainted with local conditions, especially those pertaining to the weather.

On 9 January Hitler approved these suggestions and agreed that the first German elements should cross the Danube as soon as the ice on the river could carry them. It was expected that the crossings could be effected between 10 and 15 February. By that time the Luftwaffe was to have assembled sufficient forces to provide adequate air cover. The concentration of forces for Operation **MARITA** was to be accomplished by 26 March. At that time the Italians were to pin down a maximum number of Greek forces in Albania so that only a relatively few Greek divisions would block the German thrust toward Salonika. Bulgaria was to be approached about billeting facilities for the first German elements to arrive south of the Danube.

After issuing these instructions, Hitler evaluated the overall situation in the Balkans. In his opinion Romania was the only friendly and Bulgaria the only loyal country on which the Axis Powers could rely. King Boris' hesitations in joining the Tripartite Pact were regarded as motivated only by fear of the Soviet Union, whose apparent aim it was to use Bulgaria as an assembly area for an operation leading to the seizure of the Bosporus. The greater the pressure applied by the Russians, the more likely was Bulgaria's adherence to the Tripartite Pact. Yugoslavia maintained a reserved attitude toward the Axis Powers; the leaders of that country wanted to be on the winning side without having to take any active part and were therefore playing for time.

At the beginning of January Hitler issued instructions that the Soviet Union should not be informed of German intentions in the Balkans until it made official inquiries. A few days later he changed his mind. Since rumors of an imminent German entry into Bulgaria were circulating at the time—these rumors prompted the Greek minister in Berlin to make inquiries at the Foreign Ministry and induced the Bulgarian Government to issue an official denial—Hitler deemed it advisable to forestall a Soviet *démarche*. Consequently, about 10 January the Russian ambassador in Berlin was informed of the transfer of German troops to Romania. The Soviet Union showed its concern about this information by filing a protest note in Berlin, warning Germany that the presence of foreign military forces on Bulgarian territory would be considered a threat to the security of the USSR. Hitler thereupon ordered that all discernible preparations for the Danube crossing into Bulgaria be discontinued until further notice. Although he apparently did not feel that the execution of Operation MARITA would lead to a war with Russia, he seemed to believe that the Soviet Union might attempt to incite Turkey to take up arms against Germany.

During the conferences between Hitler and Mussolini, which took place from 18 to 20 January, the Italians were fully informed about the imminent march into Bulgaria and the intended attack on Greece. On 20 January, during a review of the overall political and military situation, Hitler stated that three objectives were to be attained by the strategic concentration of German forces in Romania. First, an attack was to be launched against Greece so as to prevent the British from gaining a foothold in that country. Second, Bulgaria was to be protected against an attack by the Soviet Union and Turkey. Third, the inviolability of Romanian territory would have to be guaranteed by the presence of German forces. Each of these objectives required the formation of specific contingents of troops, and it was therefore necessary to employ very strong forces, whose assembly would take considerable time. Since it was highly desirable to effect this assembly without enemy interference, precautions had to be taken that the German plans would not be revealed prematurely. For this reason the crossing of the Danube would have to be delayed as long as possible and, once it was executed, the attack on Greece would have to be launched at the earliest moment. In all probability, Turkey would remain neutral, which would be most desirable since the consequences of Turkey joining Great Britain and placing its airfields at the latter's disposal could be quite unpleasant. Romania's internal situation was not fully clarified, but Hitler felt confident that General Antonescu would be capable of keeping it in hand.

During a conference between General Alfredo Guzzoni, the Italian Assistant Secretary of War, and Field Marshal Keitel, which took place on 19 January, the latter gained the impression that, in view of the situation in Libya and Albania, the Italians would be unable to support the German attack on Greece. On the other hand, Guzzoni asked the Germans to abstain from sending troops to Albania as planned for Operation ALPENVEILCHEN. This German plan called for the transfer of one mountain corps, composed of three divisions, to Albania. Flanked by Italian troops, these forces were to break through the Greek front at a suitable point. The plan was finally abandoned, and the Germans were thus able to concentrate their efforts on assembling forces for Operation **MARITA**.

In view of the prevailing uncertainty of Turkey's stand, the Bulgarian Government preferred not to join the Tripartite Pact before the entry of German troops on its territory. Moreover, this step was to be contingent upon the prior arrival of sufficient German antiaircraft units on Bulgarian soil.

On 28 January Hitler decided that the entry of German troops into Bulgaria was to depend upon the completion of the secret assembly of the VIII Air Corps in Romania, the establishment of adequate antiaircraft protection and coastal defenses at the ports of Varna, Constanta, and Burgas, and the provision of air cover over the Danube crossing points. The assembly of German forces in Romania was to continue without letup. The new target date for Operation MARITA—on or about 1 April—must be adhered to by the services. Antiaircraft units were not to move into Bulgaria before the other German troops. Bulgaria was not to proceed with a general mobilization before sufficient numbers of German troops had arrived in that country. The Bulgarian Air Force and antiaircraft units, as well as the civil defense organization, were to be unobtrusively alerted. German military forces were to occupy Tulcea to secure the region around the Danube estuary against seizure by the Russians.

A memorandum from the Armed Forces Operations Staff to the Foreign Ministry called special attention to the fact that no announcement of Bulgaria's adherence to the Tripartite Pact was to be made until immediately before German troops entered that country. From a military point of view it would be desirable if nonaggression pacts between Bulgaria and Turkey, Bulgaria and Yugoslavia, and Germany and Yugoslavia could be concluded before this event. The logistical problems of Operation MARITA would be greatly eased if, after the entry of German forces into Bulgaria, it would be possible to route supplies via Yugoslavia.

Upon request of the Army High Command, Hitler gave his permission to resume preparations for bridge construction on both sides of the Danube. The actual construction, however, was to be delayed as long as possible. The German forces stationed in southern Romania were to be ready to cross into Bulgaria when these preparations could no longer be kept secret. The Twelfth Army was to march from Romania into Bulgaria, move into the assembly areas along the Greek border, and simultaneously provide flank cover against a possible attack by Turkey. The Twelfth Army forces were to be divided into three echelons. The first, under the command of First Panzer Group, was to detrain in Romania by 10 February. It was to consist of three corps headquarters, and three panzer, three infantry, and one and one-half motorized infantry divisions. The second echelon was to be composed of a corps headquarters and one panzer, one infantry, and two mountain divisions, as well as one independent infantry regiment. The third echelon was to consist of one corps headquarters and six infantry divisions. The last two echelons were to detrain in Romania between 10 February and 27 March 1941.

Chapter 3

The Other Balkan Countries

I. Turkey

If Bulgaria repeatedly postponed joining the Tripartite Pact, it was primarily because of its concern over Turkish intervention. Actually, negotiations for a Bulgarian-Turkish treaty of friendship were being carried on throughout January 1941. These were progressing satisfactorily, and the terms of the treaty proposed by the

Turkish Government indicated clearly the latter's desire to keep out of the war. The signing of the treaty was announced on 17 February. Both countries stated that the immutable basis of their foreign policy was to refrain from attacking one another.

In German eyes this was by no means a guarantee that Turkey would stand aloof while German troops first entered Bulgaria and then attacked Greece, Turkey's ally. In the meantime Hitler had given his approval for bridging the Danube on 20 February; he subsequently acceded to a Bulgarian request for an eight-day postponement and set the final date as 28 February. The entry of German troops into Bulgaria was scheduled for 2 March, the day after the Bulgarian Government was to sign the Tripartite Pact. On the day the bridge construction operation was to start, the German ambassador in Ankara was to inform the Turkish Government of the impending entry of German troops into Bulgaria and of Bulgaria's decision to join the Axis Powers. Moreover, he was to announce Hitler's intention of sending a personal message to Turkey's president.

On the basis of information received from Ankara, Hitler arrived at the conclusion that the danger of Turkey's intervention had been averted. His confidence remained unshaken despite reports concerning the meetings that had taken place in Ankara on 28 February between President Ismet Inoenue and British Foreign Secretary Anthony Eden. These meetings stressed mutual respect for and adherence to the Turkish-British alliance, but apparently the British had been unsuccessful in inducing the Turks to intervene in the Balkans.

The bridge construction across the Danube began at 0700 on 28 February. At the same time, the first German unit, an antiaircraft battalion which had been assembled in southern Romania, crossed the Bulgarian border en route to Varna, where it arrived the same evening. The 5th and 11th Panzer Divisions, stationed in the Cernavoda area, were alerted to move up to the Bulgarian-Turkish border even before the general entry of German troops into Bulgaria had been effected. This turned out to be an unnecessary precaution. On 1 March Bulgaria officially joined the Tripartite Pact during a ceremony held in Vienna. On this occasion the Bulgarian premier emphasized that Bulgaria would faithfully adhere to the treaties of friendship it had previously concluded with its neighbors—in addition to the treaty just concluded with Turkey, Bulgaria had signed a treaty of friendship with Yugoslavia in 1937 and a nonaggression pact with Greece in 1938—and was determined "to maintain and further develop its traditionally friendly relations with the Soviet Union."

Figure 1. The military bridge across the Danube.

After the construction of the Danube bridges had been completed according to plan, road repair and maintenance crews were sent ahead of the German troops, which made their official entry into Bulgaria at 0600 on 2 March. The VIII Air Corps moved in simultaneously, and most of its formations arrived at the airfields near Sofiya and Plovdiv by 4 March. As soon as the bridging operation had started, all outgoing telegraph and telephone communications were stopped by German counterintelligence agents in Bulgaria, and on 2 March the Bulgarian Government closed its borders with Turkey, Greece, and Yugoslavia. The international reaction to the German entry into Bulgaria was unexpectedly mild. Great Britain broke off diplomatic relations with Bulgaria. Yugoslavia, now completely isolated, appeared more amenable to German suggestions to join the Tripartite Pact. The German minister in Athens discontinued his conversations with Greek officials; however, in conformity with Hitler's instructions diplomatic relations with Greece were not broken off. This enabled the Germans to receive reliable information from that country until shortly before they started their attack. According to reports received from Athens, motorized British and Imperial troops began to disembark at Piraeus and Volos during the first days of March.

Immediately after the German entry into Bulgaria, Turkey closed the Dardanelles and maintained a reserved attitude. On 4 March Turkey's president received Hitler's message explaining the entry of German troops into Bulgaria was the only possible solution to the predicament that confronted Germany when the British began to infiltrate Greece. Pointing to the German-Turkish alliance during World War I, Hitler emphasized his peaceful intentions toward Turkey and guaranteed that German troops would stay at least thirty-five miles from the Turkish border. In the reply, which was handed to the Fuehrer by the Turkish ambassador in Berlin in mid-March, President Inoenue also made reference to the former alliance and expressed the hope that the friendly relations existing between their two countries would be maintained in the future. After receiving this reply to his note, Hitler was no longer apprehensive of Turkey's attitude. However, in order to go one step farther and put Turkey under an obligation, Hitler contemplated giving Turkey that strip of Greek territory around Adrianople through which the Orient Express passes on its way to Istanbul.

The occupation of Bulgaria proceeded according to schedule. By 9 March the advance detachments of the leading infantry divisions had arrived at the Greek-Bulgarian border, and the 5th and 11th Panzer Divisions were fully assembled in their designated areas within fifty miles of the Turkish-Bulgarian border. Eight days later the first and second echelons, consisting of four corps headquarters, eleven and one-half divisions, and one infantry regiment, arrived on Bulgarian territory. In accordance with previous agreements, the troop contingents entering Sofiya, which the Bulgarians intended to declare an open city, consisted exclusively of service elements. The Twelfth Army under Field Marshal Wilhelm List established its headquarters south of Sofiya and directed the transfer of the German divisions to their assembly areas along the Greek-Bulgarian border.

During that time the third echelon was still detraining in Romania. As early as 7 March the Army High Command arrived at the conclusion that, in view of Turkey's more and more favorable attitude toward the German occupation of Bulgaria, it would be advisable to keep the six infantry divisions of this echelon in Romania so that they would be promptly available for Operation BARBAROSSA and would not be exhausted by long marches.

II. Yugoslavia

Throughout this period Yugoslavia had successfully avoided being drawn into the Italian-Greek conflict. Hitler's policy was to induce the Yugoslav political leaders to collaborate with Germany and Italy. On 28 November 1940, during a conference with Yugoslavia's Foreign Minister Lazar Cincar-Marcovic, the Fuehrer offered to sign a nonaggression pact with Yugoslavia and recommended its adherence to the Tripartite Pact. Hitler mentioned on that occasion that he intended to intervene in the Balkans by assisting the Italians against Greece. Once the British forces had been driven out of the Balkans, frontier corrections would have to be made, and Yugoslavia might be given an outlet to the Aegean Sea through Salonika. Although Cincar-Marcovic seemed impressed by these arguments, no further progress was made.

During the planning for Operation MARITA, German military leaders pointed repeatedly to Yugoslavia's crucial position and asked that diplomatic pressure be used to induce that country to join the Axis Powers. Because of the lack of direct rail lines between Bulgaria and Greece, the use of the Brigade-Nis-Salonika rail line was essential for the rapid execution of Operation MARITA and the speedy redeployment of forces for Operation BARBAROSSA.

On 14 February 1941 Hitler and Foreign Minister Joachim von Ribbentrop met with the Yugoslav Premier Dragisha Cvetkovic and Cincar-Marcovic. For the Germans the results were as unsatisfactory as those of the preceding meeting, since the conference did not lead to the conclusion of any agreement. D-day for Operation MARITA was drawing closer and Yugoslavia still refused to commit itself. Hitler therefore invited Prince Regent Paul to continue the negotiations, and a meeting took place on 4 March. The prince regent's reaction to the German desiderata was much more favorable than that of the political leaders whom Hitler had met before. However, in strict pursuance of Yugoslavia's policy of neutrality, Prince Paul declined to give the Axis Powers any military support, intimating that this would be incompatible with Yugoslav public opinion. Hitler assured him that he fully appreciated the regent's difficulties and guaranteed him that, even after adhering to the Tripartite Pact, Yugoslavia would not be required to permit the transit of German troops across its territory. Although the military considered the use of the Yugoslav rail net as essential, Hitler attached so much political weight to Yugoslavia's adherence to the Tripartite Pact that he would not let that point interfere with the successful conclusion of the pending negotiations. Moreover, he hoped that the Yugoslav Government could eventually be induced to reverse its decision and permit the transit of German supply and materiel shipments across its territory.

For the time being, however, the negotiations with Yugoslavia made little progress, in spite of Hitler's willingness to make concessions. Yugoslav opposition to Italy's interference in the Balkans seemed to be the chief obstacle. By mid-March the situation had reached the point where Mussolini decided to order the reinforcement of the garrisons along the Italian-Yugoslav border. On 18 March the situation suddenly took a turn for the better—the Yugoslav privy council decided to join the Tripartite Pact. The ceremony took place in Vienna on 25 March, when Cvetkovic and Cincar-Marcovic signed the protocol. On this occasion the Axis Powers handed two notes to the Yugoslav representatives. In these they guaranteed to respect the sovereignty and territorial integrity of Yugoslavia at all times and promised that, for the duration of the war, Yugoslavia would not be required to permit the transit of Axis troops across its territory.

Hitler's triumph over this diplomatic success was, however, short-lived. During the night of 26–27 March a military *coup d'état* at Belgrade led to the resignation of the existing government and the formation of a new one headed by General Richard D. Simovic, the former commander of the Yugoslav Air Force. Simultaneously, the seventeen-year-old King Peter II acceded to the throne and Prince Regent Paul and his family departed for Greece. The frontiers of Yugoslavia were hermetically sealed. Anti-German demonstrations were held in Belgrade and several other Serbian cities and, on 29 March, the Yugoslav Army was mobilized.

Although a nationalistic wave of enthusiasm swept the entire country with the exception of Croatia, the realities of the military situation gave little reason for optimism. Yugoslavia was surrounded by Axis forces except for the narrow strip of common border with Greece. The situation of the Yugoslav Army was rendered particularly difficult by the shortage of modern weapons. Moreover, since most of its equipment had been produced in Germany or in armament plants under German control, it was impossible to renew the supply of ammunition.

On 27 March the new Yugoslav foreign minister immediately assured the German minister in Belgrade that his country wanted to maintain its friendly relations with Germany. Although it would not ratify its adherence to the Tripartite Pact, Yugoslavia did not want to cancel any standing agreements. Despite this information Hitler was convinced that the new government was anti-German and opposed to the pact and that Yugoslavia would sooner or later join the Western Powers. He therefore called a meeting of the commanders in chief of the Army and Luftwaffe and their chiefs of staff, Ribbentrop, Keitel, and Generaloberst (General) Alfred Jodl for 1300 on 27 March. He informed them that he had decided to "destroy Yugoslavia as a military power and sovereign state." This would have to be accomplished with a minimum of delay and with the assistance of those nations that had borders in common with Yugoslavia. Italy, Hungary, and to a certain extent Bulgaria, would have to lend direct military support, whereas Romania's principal role was to block any attempts at Soviet intervention. The annihilation of the Yugoslav state would have to be executed in blitzkrieg manner. The three services would be responsible for making the necessary preparations with utmost speed.

Following these explanations Hitler issued the overall instructions for the execution of the operation against Yugoslavia and asked the commanders in chief of the Army and Luftwaffe to submit their plans without delay. These instructions were laid down in Directive No. 25, which was signed by Hitler the same evening and immediately issued to the services.

In a telegram sent to Mussolini on 27 March, Hitler informed the Italian chief of state that he had made all preparations "to meet a critical development by taking the necessary military countermeasures," and that he had acquainted the Hungarian and Bulgarian ministers with his views on the situation in an attempt to rouse the interest of their respective governments to lending military support. Moreover, he asked the Duce "not to start any new ventures in Albania during the next few days" but "to cover the most important passes leading from Yugoslavia to Albania with all available forces and to quickly reinforce the Italian troops along the Italian-Yugoslav border."

A written confirmation of this telegram was handed to Mussolini the next day and negotiations regarding Italy's participation in a war against Yugoslavia were initiated immediately. The Germans

submitted a memorandum containing suggestions to promote the coordination of the German and Italian operations against Yugoslavia. The memorandum outlined the German plans and assigned the following missions to the Italian forces:
  a. To protect the flank of the German attack forces, which were to be assembled around Graz, by moving all immediately available ground forces in the direction of Split and Jajce;
  b. To switch to the defensive along the Greek-Albanian front and assemble an attack force, which was to link up with the Germans driving toward Skoplje and points farther south;
  c. To neutralize the Yugoslav naval forces in the Adriatic;
  d. To resume the offensive on the Greek front in Albania at a later date.

Mussolini approved the German plans and instructed General Guzzoni to comply with them. As a result, the Italian army group in Albania diverted four divisions to the protection of the eastern and northern borders of that country where they faced Yugoslavia.

No definite agreement had been made about possible cooperation between the German and Italian naval forces in the war against Greece. At the beginning of March, during a conversation between General Guzzoni and the German liaison officer with the Italian armed forces, the former had emphasized the necessity of defining the German and Italian military objectives in the Balkans and of assigning liaison staffs to the field commands. However, because of continued Italian reverses in Albania, Hitler was not interested in any such agreement. Finally, he decided that liaison officers might be exchanged between Twelfth Army and the Italian commander in Albania. The Italians were not supposed to know any details of Operation MARITA or its target date until six days before D-day.

When first approached, the Hungarians showed little enthusiasm for participating in the campaign against Yugoslavia. They made no immediate military preparations, but gave their permission for the assembly of one German corps near the western Hungarian border southwest of Lake Balaton.

Romanian units were to guard the Romanian-Yugoslav border and, together with the German military mission stationed in that country, provide rear guard protection against an attack by the Soviet Union. Antonescu was greatly concerned over the possibility of Russian intervention in the Balkans as soon as Germany invaded Yugoslavia. His apprehensions were based on rumors regarding the signing of a mutual-assistance pact between the Soviet Union and Yugoslavia. Hitler tried to reassure him by promising maximum German support and ordering the immediate reinforcement of the German antiaircraft artillery units in Romania and the transfer of additional firefighting forces to the oil region.

King Boris of Bulgaria refused to lend active support in the campaigns against Greece and Yugoslavia. He pointed out that by 15 April only five Bulgarian divisions would be available for deployment along the Turkish border and that he could not possibly commit any forces elsewhere.

On 3 April a Yugoslav delegation arrived in Moscow to sign a pact of mutual assistance with the Soviet Union. Instead, they signed a treaty of friendship and nonaggression two days later. By concluding this treaty the Soviet Government apparently wanted to show its interest in Yugoslavia and the Balkans without much hope that this gesture would induce Hitler to reconsider his decision to attack Yugoslavia. The next day, 6 April 1941, the Luftwaffe unleashed an air attack on Belgrade and the German Army started to invade Yugoslavia.

PART TWO
THE YUGOSLAV CAMPAIGN
(Operation 25)

Chapter 4
Political and Strategic Planning

Upon his assumption of power on 27 March 1941, General Simovic, the new head of the Yugoslav Government, was faced with a difficult situation. Realizing that Germany was making feverish preparations to invade Yugoslavia, he tried his utmost to unify his government by including representative Croat elements. It was not until 3 April—just three days before the German attack was launched—that the Croat leaders finally joined the Simovic government. Upon entering the cabinet, Croat representatives appealed to their people to give the new regime wholehearted support. However, any semblance of national solidarity was to be short lived. When Croatia proclaimed itself an independent state with Hitler's blessings on 10 April, the Croat political leaders promptly left the national government in Belgrade and returned to Zagreb. Thus the cleft in Yugoslavia's national unity, superficially closed for exactly seven days, became complete.

While the Simovic government made every effort to maintain friendly relations with Germany, Hitler was bent on settling the issue by force of arms. Preparations for the rapid conquest of Yugoslavia were hastened so as not to jeopardize the impending campaign against Russia. Germany's limited resources precluded the possibility of tying down forces in Yugoslavia for any protracted period while simultaneously invading the Soviet Union.

The possibility of an invasion of Yugoslavia had hitherto not been considered by the German Army planners. For a better understanding of the problems with which the German General Staff officers were faced, it is necessary to examine the topographic features of that country.

I. Military Topography

Geographically, the Balkans extend from the Danube to the Aegean and from the Black Sea to the Adriatic. (Map 1) Mountain ranges and narrow, mountain-lined valleys are characteristic of the Balkan peninsula, of which Yugoslavia constitutes the northwestern and central portion. Central Yugoslavia is a plateau that slopes gently toward the Danube Valley and gradually merges into the Hungarian plains.

The Yugoslav coastline along the Adriatic extends for approximately 400 miles and is fronted by numerous small islands. The Dalmatian Alps, which run along the coast, constitute a formidable barrier as good roads are scarce. Stretching across the peninsula, roughly from east to west, are the Balkan Mountains. The ranges are high, rough, and rugged, and are intersticed by numerous passes which, however, can be successfully negotiated by specially trained and equipped mountain troops.

The inland frontiers of Yugoslavia extend some 1,900 miles and border on Italy, Austria, Hungary, Romania, Bulgaria, Greece, and Albania. Covering a land surface approximately the size of the State of Oregon, Yugoslavia has a population of almost 16 million, of which 5 million Serbs and 3 million Croats constitute the two largest ethnic groups. In the northern part of the country a German minority element numbers about half a million. The largest cities are Belgrade, the national capital, with 400,000 inhabitants, and Zagreb, the principal Croat city, with 200,000.

The country can be roughly divided into five distinct natural geographic regions. The so-called Pannonian Basin, within which the national capital of Belgrade is centrally located, is by far the most important industrial portion. The Sava and Drava valleys link this area with the Slovene Alps, the forerunners of the more formidable Julian Alps. The Morava-Vardar depression extends southward from Belgrade to the Greek frontier. The Adriatic coastal belt extends from Italy in the north to Albania in the south. The Dalmatian Alps rise directly out of the sea and overshadow the central mountain or Dinaric Karst region farther inland.

There are several great routes of communication in the Balkans. One of these follows the Morava and Vardar Rivers from Budapest to Salonika and connects the Danube with the Aegean. The best roads and railroad lines are to be found in the northern and northeastern fringes of Yugoslavia which formed part of the Austro-Hungarian Empire.

Because of its difficult terrain, Yugoslavia is far from being ideally suited for the conduct of major military operations. This poorly developed, rugged, and mountainous country, with its limited routes of communication and sparsely populated area, is bound to raise havoc with an invader's communications, movements, and logistical support.

Almost all of the rivers, including the Drava, Sava, and Morava, are tributaries of the Danube, which flows through the northwestern part of Yugoslavia for about 350 miles. Soon after crossing the northern border an attacking ground force is confronted by three formidable river barriers: the Mura, the Drava, and the Sava. At the time of the spring thaws these rivers resemble swollen torrents; the Drava at Barcs and the lower course of the Sava become as wide as the Mississippi at St. Louis. It is therefore of vital importance for the invader to seize the key bridges across these rivers while they are still intact.

II. Hitler's Concept of the Strategic Factors

During the conference that took place on the afternoon of 27 March 1941, Hitler formulated overall strategic plans for the projected military operation against Yugoslavia. The decisions reached at this meeting were summarized in Directive No. 25, which was disseminated to the three armed services on the same day. The campaign against Yugoslavia took its cover name—Operation 25—from this directive.

Hitler declared that the uprising in Yugoslavia had drastically changed the entire political situation in the Balkans. He maintained that Yugoslavia must now be regarded as an enemy and must be destroyed as quickly as possible despite any assurances that might be forthcoming from the new Yugoslav Government. Hungary and Bulgaria were to be induced to participate in the operations by extending to them the opportunity of regaining Banat and Macedonia, respectively. By the same token, political promises were to be extended to the Croats, promises that were bound to have all the more telling effect since they would render even more acute the internal dissension within Yugoslavia.

In view of Yugoslavia's difficult terrain, the German plans called for a two-pronged drive in the general direction of Belgrade, with one assault force coming from southeastern Austria and the other from western Bulgaria. These forces were to crush the Yugoslav armed forces in the north. Simultaneously, the southernmost part of Yugoslavia was to be used as a jumpoff area for a combined German-Italian offensive against Greece. Vital as the early capture of Belgrade proper was considered to be, possession of the Belgrade–Nis–Salonika rail line and highway and of the Danube waterway was of

Figure 2. Bridge across the Drava River damaged by the Yugoslavs.

even greater strategic importance to the German supply system. Hitler therefore arrived at the following conclusions:

1. As soon as sufficient forces became available and the weather conditions permitted, the Luftwaffe was to destroy the city of Belgrade as well as the ground installations of the Yugoslav Air Force by means of uninterrupted day-and-night bombing attacks. The launching of Operation MARITA was to coincide with the initial air bombardment.

2. All forces already available in Bulgaria and Romania could be utilized for the ground attacks, one to be launched toward Belgrade from the Sofiya region, the other toward Skoplje from the Kyustendil–Gorna Dzhumaya area. However, approximately one division and sufficient antiaircraft elements must remain in place to protect the vital Romanian oil fields. The guarding of the Turkish frontier was to be left to the Bulgarians for the time being, but, if practicable, one armored division was to be kept in readiness behind the Bulgarian frontier security forces.

3. The attack from Austria toward the southeast was to be launched as soon as the necessary forces could be assembled in the Graz area. The ultimate decision as to whether Hungarian soil should be used for staging the drive against Yugoslavia was to be left to the Army. Security forces along the northern Yugoslav frontier were to be reinforced at once. Even before the main attacks could be launched, crucial points should be seized and made secure along the northern and eastern Yugoslav border. Any such limited-objective attacks were to be so timed as to coincide with the air bombardment of Belgrade.

4. The Luftwaffe was to lend tactical support and cover during the ground operations in the vicinity of the Yugoslav border and coordinate its efforts with the requirements of the Army. Adequate antiaircraft protection was to be provided in the vital concentration areas around Graz, Klagenfurt, Villach, Leoben, and Vienna.

Chapter 5

The Plan of Attack

I. The Outline Plan

Working under tremendous pressure, the Army High Command developed the combined outline plan for the Yugoslav and Greek campaigns within twenty-four hours of the military revolt in Yugoslavia.

After this plan had been submitted to and approved by Hitler, it was incorporated into Directive No. 25.

This outline plan envisaged the following offensive operations:

1. One attack force was to drive southward from the former Austrian province of Styria and from southwestern Hungary. This force was to destroy the enemy armies in Croatia and drive southeastward between the Sava and Drava Rivers toward Belgrade. The mobile divisions of this assault group were to coordinate their advance with the other attack forces that were to close in on the Yugoslav capital from other directions so that the bulk of the enemy forces would be unable to make an orderly withdrawal into the mountains.

2. The second force was to advance toward Belgrade from the Sofiya area in western Bulgaria, take the capital, and secure the Danube so that river traffic could be reopened at an early date.

3. A third attack force was to thrust from southwestern Bulgaria in the general direction of Skoplje in an effort to cut off the Yugoslav Army from the Greek and British forces, while at the same time easing the precarious situation of the Italians in Albania.

4. Finally, elements of the German Twelfth Army, which were poised and ready to invade Greece from Bulgarian bases and had the difficult task of surmounting the hazardous terrain fortified by the Metaxas Line, were to pass through the southern tip of Yugoslavia, execute an enveloping thrust via the Vardar Valley toward Salonika, and thus ease the task of the German forces that were conducting the frontal assault against the Greek fortified positions.

II. The Timing of the Attacks

In its original version, the outline plan for Operation 25 called for the air bombardment of Belgrade and the ground installations of the Yugoslav Air Force to take place on 1 April, the invasion of Greece—Operation MARITA—on 2 or 3 April, and ground attacks against Yugoslavia between 8 and 15 April.

During the afternoon of 29 March the Deputy Chief of Staff for Operations, Generalleutnant (Major General) Friedrich Paulus—who was to lead the survivors of the Stalingrad pocket into Russian captivity less than two years later—presided over a special conference in Vienna at which the plans of attack and timetable for the operations against Greece and Yugoslavia were discussed. Present with their respective chiefs of staff were Field Marshal List, the commander of Twelfth Army, Generaloberst (General) Maximilian von Weichs of Second Army, and Generaloberst (General) Ewald von Kleist of the First Panzer Group. Field Marshal List was brought up to date on the changes in the situation necessitated by the Yugoslav campaign, and all commanders were fully briefed on the projected plans for the conduct of the operations. Decisions were reached as to which units were to participate in the various thrusts from Austria and Hungary under the command of Second Army. In addition, the corps headquarters and GHQ units were selected and assigned.

One of the subjects discussed during this meeting was the participation of Germany's allies and satellites in the Yugoslav campaign. Since the Italians in Albania had demonstrated their inability to mount any offensive operations and the Italian Second Army deployed in northern Italy apparently would not be ready for action until 22 April, any real assistance from that side was not to be expected. At any rate, according to the German Army Command plans, the Yugoslav operations would be almost completed by the time the Italians could be ready. The Hungarians acceded to all German requests for the use of their territory and agreed to take an active part in the operations by committing contingents, which were to be subordinated to the German Army High Command. At the conclusion of the conference, General Paulus proceeded to Budapest to discuss details of the operation with the Hungarian general staff.

Another result of the conference of 29 March was the decision to delay the initial air attacks so that they would coincide more closely with the attack on Greece. The purpose of this measure was to bring Operation MARITA into a closer relationship with Operation 25. The revised timetable thus foresaw that the attacks of Twelfth Army to the south and west and the air bombardment would be launched simultaneously on 6 April, the thrust of First Panzer Group on 8 April, and the Second Army attack on 12 April. These deadlines were adhered to with the exception of D-day for Second Army, which was moved up when the rapid successes scored by the probing attacks led to the decision of getting off to a "flying start."

III. Second Army

In the final version of the plan of attack the Second Army was to jumpoff on 10 April with its mobile forces driving in the general direction of Belgrade between the Drava and Sava Rivers. The terrain between the two rivers was considered ideal for armored warfare, and no serious obstacles were expected. The army was greatly concerned, however, over the prospect of finding key bridges demolished, especially since little bridging equipment was available and the rivers were swollen by spring thaws. For this reason the lead elements of the XLVI Panzer Corps were to conduct limited objective attacks as early as 6 April in order to seize and secure the highway and railroad bridges across the Drava near Barcs. In this manner the corps would be able to launch its thrust toward Belgrade by 8 April, the same time that the First Panzer Group was to attack from the southeast. One motorized column was to be diverted to the southwest with the mission of capturing Zagreb at the earliest possible moment.

Farther to the west, where the terrain becomes more and more mountainous, the LI Infantry Corps was to jumpoff on 10 April and drive in the direction of Zagreb with two infantry divisions. Here, too, limited objective attacks were to be carried out during the preceding days so that strategic points in the proximity of the frontier could be secured.

On the same day, and as soon as sufficient troops became available, the XLIX Mountain Corps was to advance toward Celje.

IV. First Panzer Group

In compliance with Directive No. 25, Field Marshal List's Twelfth Army, which had originally been assembled in Bulgaria for the purpose of executing Operation MARITA, had to regroup its divisions into three separate attack forces. The plan of attack of the southern and central forces will be dealt with in Part III, "The German Campaign in Greece." The northern attack force of Twelfth Army, led by General von Kleist's First Panzer Group, was to launch a surprise attack in the direction of Nis–Kragujevac–Belgrade on 8 April, annihilate strong enemy forces concentrated in the Pirot-Leskovac sector, and capture the Yugoslav capital with a minimum of delay.

The First Panzer Group forces had to be reorganized and regrouped for their new mission. By using every available motor vehicle, the regrouping could be achieved within a few days. For this purpose, motor vehicles from German forces stationed in Romania and from the 16th Panzer Division, deployed behind the Bulgarian-Turkish border, had to be organized into makeshift motor transport columns and hurriedly pressed into service. The forces at the disposal of the panzer group were comparatively weak, considering the difficulties they were bound to encounter. In all probability, the Yugoslavs would concentrate their best troops in the vicinity of the capital, which was not easily accessible from the southeast. The German armor would be forced to negotiate some formidable mountain roads before reaching its objective. Thus, in the event that the Serbs established a well-organized defense system, this attack might involve considerable risk.

V. XLI Panzer Corps

To coincide with this thrust, the XLI Panzer Corps, which was assembling in western Romania, was to undertake a separate drive from the Timisoara area to Belgrade. The outline plan did not envision the employment of the XLI Panzer Corps during the Yugoslav campaign. However, without consulting the Army High Command, Hitler ordered the 2d SS Motorized Infantry Division to advance on Belgrade from Timisoara. He apparently wanted an SS division to be the first to enter the Yugoslav capital, both for prestige reasons and propaganda purposes. Upon learning of this move, the Army High Command protested vigorously and soon obtained complete operational control over this force, which subsequently formed the third prong in the drive on Belgrade.

Chapter 6

The Defense Forces

I. General

Lacking up-to-date materiel, the Yugoslav armed forces were no match for the well-equipped and highly trained German war machine. Their deficiencies were particularly marked in the fields of aviation and armor. In January 1941 the Yugoslav Air Force numbered approximately 700 military aircraft, most of which were obsolete. A major portion of all weapons and equipment was of foreign make, with the Skoda armament plant the main source. After the Germans annexed the whole of Czechoslovakia in 1939, deliveries from that source ceased almost completely. In the opinion of some German military experts the pronounced inferiority of Yugoslav equipment and material was partly compensated for by the inaccessibility of the country and toughness of the individual soldier. However, internal friction among the different ethnic groups, particularly between Serbs and Croats, undermined the overall combat effectiveness of the Yugoslav military forces.

II. Defensive Plans

The Yugoslav plan of defense called for a fairly even distribution of all available forces along the extended frontiers of the country. In adopting a cordon defense the Yugoslav high command displayed little ingenuity as it deprived itself of the opportunity of forming strong reserves. Since the capital of Belgrade and the industrial area around Nis and Kragujevac were situated so close to the frontier, major elements of the Army were tied down in the defense of those

Figure 3. Yugoslav obstacles across the railway tracks near Spielfeld.

sectors. Moreover, the Yugoslav command intended to maintain contact with the Greek and British troops in Greece by strengthening its forces in northern Macedonia. In conjunction with a Greek attack from the south, the Yugoslav high command planned to commit the Third Army in a drive against Albania from the east. While this attack force was to push the Italians out of Albania, the other armies were to fight delaying actions if any frontier sector should be invaded by Germany. In the event of initial setbacks in the border areas, the Yugoslavs intended to conduct an orderly withdrawal into the inaccessible mountainous regions in the western part of the country, where they hoped to continue their resistance by engaging the invader in costly and timeconsuming guerilla warfare.

This plan was unrealistic and therefore bound to fail. The Yugoslav Army could have escaped total annihilation only if it had operated in conjunction with the Greek and British forces and had built up a line of resistance in the extreme southern part of the country to achieve this purpose. This line should have been anchored on the Greek front in Albania in the west and on the mountains along the Greek-Bulgarian frontier in the east. This would have meant the voluntary abandonment of almost the entire national territory, a decision which no Yugoslav political leader could possibly have envisaged.

III. Training and Tactics

Combined-arms training and maneuvers under simulated combat conditions had been seriously neglected by the Yugoslavs. During training much emphasis was placed on delaying actions, defensive fighting, and the conduct of counterattacks. Considerable weight was also attached to assault tactics of infantry forces. The individual Serb soldier was well trained in close-combat and hand-to-hand fighting, but was powerless against heavy artillery fire and air-supported armored thrusts.

IV. Guerilla Warfare

Special emphasis was placed on guerilla warfare, for which the Serbs were especially well suited and trained. The "Cetnici," a partisan organization composed of loyal Serbs, had been formed into militia units of varying size up to battalion strength. Its primary mission was to carry out raids and acts of sabotage against enemy command posts and rear area installations. Guerilla units were to be committed to reinforce the frontier guards so that they could wage their specialized type of warfare against an attacker from the very outset of operations.

V. Fortifications

There was no continuous line of fortifications along the Yugoslav frontier. Although pillboxes had been constructed in certain places to reinforce individual strong points, these were at best interconnected by unimproved, open trenches. None of the pillboxes had armor-plated cupolas; they were armed primarily with machine guns and, in some instances, with antitank and light artillery guns. Though these fortified positions were far from imposing, they were, as a rule, well concealed and camouflaged. Several rows of wire entanglements protected the positions. At some points tank obstacles and antitank ditches were built in front of the fortified lines. The obstacles consisted of from three to five rows of steel girders which had merely been driven into the ground but were not anchored in a concrete foundation. Consequently, they did not constitute a formidable barrier for the modern-type medium tank. The antitank ditches, though few in number, were well conceived and effectively constructed. They measured twenty-four feet in width and nine feet in depth, and their steep retaining wall was revetted.

Because of the mountainous terrain along the German-Yugoslav frontier, the defense system in this area was limited to blocking main roads and key mountain passes where a German penetration was most likely to occur. It was here that most of the fortified positions had been constructed. Their size and strength varied depending on the importance of the border-crossing point and on the natural terrain features.

VI. Order of Battle

At the beginning of April 1941 the Yugoslav Army was composed of seventeen regular and twelve reserve infantry divisions, six combined-arms brigades, three regular cavalry divisions and three reserve cavalry brigades, one fortress division, and one fortress brigade. There were also twenty-three frontier guard battalions, a number of frontier guard regiments, and some fortification troops. The fully mobilized strength of the Army was slightly under 1,000,000 men.

The divisions and brigades were not designated numerically, as is normally the case, but were named after provinces, rivers, mountain ranges, or cities. They were organized into three army groups, seven field armies, and one coastal defense command. The following were their composition and primary missions on 6 April 1941:

    1. The First Army Group consisted of: the Seventh Army, including two infantry divisions, two mountain brigades, and one coastal defense battalion, was responsible for the defense of the

northwestern part of the country facing the Italian and German frontiers; the Fourth Army, composed of three infantry divisions and one cavalry brigade, was to hold the sector facing the Hungarian border, and was deployed behind the Drava from Varazdin to Slatina. Behind this defense line a cavalry division stood in reserve in the Zagreb area, while three additional infantry divisions were held in reserve south of the Croat capital.

2. The Second Army Group was composed of: the Second Army including three infantry divisions holding the sector adjacent to Fourth Army up to the Danube; one additional infantry division which was located south of Brod and formed the army reserve; and the First Army, which consisted of one cavalry and two infantry divisions, and occupied the northwest corner between the Danube and the Tisza.

3. The Sixth Army was an independent command not subordinated to an army group. It was composed of two infantry divisions, one infantry brigade, one reinforced cavalry division, and one reinforced cavalry brigade. These forces were deployed around Belgrade and in the Banat region east of the Tisza. Two additional infantry divisions were upheld in reserve along both banks of the lower Morava Valley.

4. The Third Army Group consisted of: the Fifth Army, which had four infantry divisions and two infantry brigades to cover the Romanian border from the Iron Gate up to Kriva Palanka; three additional infantry divisions under the army's jurisdiction covered the adjacent sector to the south, extending to the Greek frontier; and the Third Army, composed of four infantry divisions and one separate battalion, which was deployed along the Albanian border from Lake Ohridsko to Lake Shadarsko. One infantry division was held in reserve in the Skoplje area.

5. The Coastal Defense Command had at its disposal one infantry division as well as the Kotorski Fortress Division and the Sibenik Fortress Brigade. This command was responsible for the defense of the Adriatic coast from the Bay of Kotorski to Gospic.

VII. Deficiencies and Confusion

Because of the political situation, the inadequate rail and road nets, and the poor organization of the Army as a whole, the Yugoslav defense forces were committed piecemeal. The frontier defenses, although built around favorable terrain features, lacked depth and usually confined themselves to the immediate border environs.

When hostilities began on 6 April, the Yugoslav Army was still in the midst of mobilization, with sizable forces being clothed and equipped in their garrisons. As a result, the disposition of troops behind the 1,900-mile border was totally inadequate. The only units that were fully mobilized were the regular Army divisions of the Third and Fifth Armies, which were stationed along the Bulgarian border. Some of the border security battalions were on a war footing, but even they were understrength. Not until 3 April did the Yugoslavs start to shift troop units from the interior to the Bulgarian frontier. No strategic reserves whatsoever were available in the Ljubljana area in the north.

During his discussions with Yugoslav leaders in Belgrade on 1 April, General Sir John Dill, Chief of the British Imperial General Staff, found nothing but confusion and paralysis. Political leaders repeatedly stated that Yugoslavia was determined not to take any steps that might provoke a German armed attack. Obviously, the Yugoslav ministers failed to realize the imminence of their country's peril. Their mood and outlook left Dill under the impression that they believed they would have months to make their decisions and enforce their plans, whereas in reality only a few days were to elapse before the Germans launched their attack.

Chapter 7

The Attack Forces

I. Command Posts

On 5 April Field Marshall Walther von Brauchitsch, Commander in Chief of the Germany Army, moved to Wiener Neustadt (thirty-five miles south of Vienna) in order to assume personal command of the Second and Twelfth Armies, which were to conduct the campaigns against Yugoslavia and Greece. He was accompanied by an advance echelon of the Army General Staff. Reichs Marshal Goering, Commander in Chief of the Luftwaffe, established his field headquarters at Semmering Pass, southwest of Wiener Neustadt.

Accompanied by his close entourage and the forward echelon of the National Defense Branch of the Armed Forces Operations Staff, Hitler departed from Berlin on the evening of 10 April. On the following day the Fuehrer arrived at a small station on the single-track railroad line leading from Wiener Neustadt southward to Fuerstenberg (fifty miles east of Graz). There, his special train and that of the National Defense Branch halted in front of the northern and southern exits respectively of a tunnel that leads through the Alps south of Aspang.

From these locations the trains could easily be pulled into the tunnel in the event of enemy air attacks. While the two trains remained in the area, the entire line was blocked to normal traffic. It was from this vantage point that Hitler directed the Balkan campaigns until 25 April, when he returned to Berlin.

II. The Luftwaffe

The ground operations in the Balkans were to be given strong and effective air support by the Fourth Air Force under the command of General der Flieger (Lieutenant General) Alexander Loehr, whose headquarters was then located in Vienna. The actual air operations were carried out by the VIII Air Corps of General der Flieger (Lieutenant General) Wolfram von Richthofen. It was he who had established such an outstanding record in supporting the slashing armored thrusts during the Battle of France.

Between November 1940 and February 1941, a force of over 400 planes, including long-range bombers, dive-bombers, fighters, and reconnaissance aircraft, had gradually been built up in Romania and Bulgaria. By 27 March, when the Yugoslav revolt occurred, there were 135 fighter and reconnaissance planes in Romania, and 355 bombers and dive-bombers in Bulgaria.

Early in April additional air reinforcements were rushed to the Balkans. From as far away as France, Africa, and Sicily about 600 aircraft of all four types were brought up and readied for action within ten days. The fighter and reconnaissance craft were sent to fields near Arad, Deva, and Turnu-Severin in western Romania, all within easy striking distance of Belgrade. The long-range bombers were to operate from fields at Wiener Neustadt and near Sofiya, northwest and southeast of the Yugoslav capital, at 200 and 100 miles distance, respectively.

III. Second Army

The disposition and order of battle of the various attack groups under Second Army were as follows (appendix I):

1. The XLIX Mountain Corps under General der Infanterie (Lieutenant General) Ludwig Kuebler was assembled in the Klagenfurt area. The only two divisions originally assigned to this corps were the 1st Mountain and the 538th Frontier Guard Divisions.

2. The LI Infantry Corps of General der Infanterie (Lieutenant General) Hans Reinhardt moved into the Leibnitz area. This corps composed of the 101st Light Infantry and 132d and 183d Infantry Divisions, was to form the main effort of the southward thrust.

Figure 4. German supply column crossing a 4,100-foot pass in Bulgaria.

3. The LII Infantry Corps, under the command of General der Infanterie (Lieutenant General) Kurt von Briesen, consisted of two infantry divisions, the 79th and 125th, which were supposed to be committed alongside LI Corps. Since these forces did not arrive in time and were eventually not needed for the operation, they were placed in the Army High Command reserve.

4. XLVI Panzer Corps, under the command of General der Panzertruppen (Lieutenant General) Heinrich von Vietinghoff, was assembled in southwestern Hungary near Nagykanizsa. It was composed of the 8th and 14th Panzer Divisions and the 16th Motorized Infantry Division.

IV. First Panzer Group

The First Panzer Group headquarters under General von Kleist had originally been designated to command the spearhead divisions in the campaign against Greece. After the revision of plans the following units were assigned to the panzer group and diverted to participate in the Yugoslav campaign:

1. The XIV Panzer Corps, under the command of General der Infanterie (Lieutenant General) Gustav von Wietersheim, composed of the 5th and 11th Panzer, the 294th Infantry, and the 4th Mountain Divisions.

2. The XI Infantry Corps, under the command of General der Infanterie (Lieutenant General) Joachim von Kortzfleisch, consisted of the 60th Motorized Infantry Division and several other units which, however, did not participate in the campaign.

V. XLI Panzer Corps

An independent armored corps, the XLI Panzer Corps, was assembled in western Romania near Timisoara under the command of General der Panzertruppen (Lieutenant General) Georg-Hans Reinhardt. It comprised the 2d SS Motorized Infantry Division, the reinforced Motorized Infantry Regiment "Gross Deutschland," and the Panzer Regiment "Hermann Goering."

Chapter 8

Logistical Planning and Assembly of Second Army

I. The Rail Transportation Problem

The forces assigned to Second Army had to be shifted from France and Germany as well as from the Russian border. (Map 3) In accordance with the schedule for the concentration of forces for Operation BARBAROSSA, large-scale movements to Germany's eastern border were under way toward the end of March. Consequently, the Second Army forces that were designated to participate in the Yugoslav campaign had to be rerouted toward the south, some of them even in the midst of their west-east movement. Several efficient railroad lines running from north to south were available for the movement. Two of these lines led to Vienna, one via Breslau and the other via Munich, Salzburg, and Linz. Two additional lines terminated in Passau, one via Nuremberg and the other via Munich. The line from Prague via Pilsen to Vienna was also available but had only a limited capacity.

The movements from Vienna and Passau through the Alps into the detraining areas around Graz and into western Hungary presented more complicated problems. Since the capacities of the feeder lines and detraining points were considered inadequate, some elements were forced to detrain in Vienna and Salzburg and continue the movement to the assembly areas by road.

The Graz area and western Styria were particularly difficult to reach. Here, the feeder lines traversed the Alps and were consequently of very limited capacity. For this reason it became imperative to include the western tip of Hungary as as assembly area for some of the German attack forces. After Hungary had agreed to the use of its territory, the assembly of the German Second Army proceeded as follows:

1. Graz and western Styria were designated as assembly areas for all infantry divisions. Three railroad lines with the following daily feeder capacity were available in those areas:

a. The daily capacity of the line Vienna–Bruck–Graz was sixty trains from Vienna to Bruck and forty-eight from Bruck to Graz. However, only fifty-two military trains could be dispatched from Vienna to Bruck since eight trains destined for Italy were needed daily to haul coal over that stretch. These trains had to be kept running on schedule so that the German concentrations could be concealed from the Yugoslavs as long as possible.

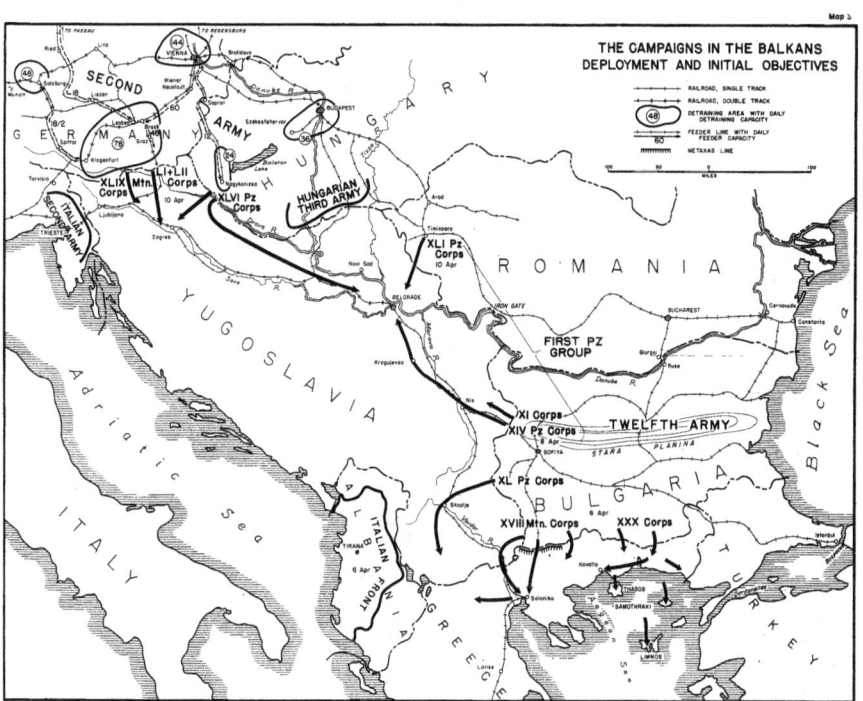

b. The line Passau–Ried–Leoben had a carrying capacity of eighteen trains.

c. The line Salzburg–Spittal–Klagenfurt could also carry eighteen trains daily, but only with half the normal load because of the steep gradients across the Alps.

The daily detraining capacity of the Bruck–Graz–Klagenfurt area was seventy-eight trains, or the equivalent of the combat elements of two infantry divisions. Consequently, all of the rear echelon elements of these divisions had to detrain in the Vienna area, capable of handling 144 trains a day, and in Salzburg, where forty-eight additional trains could be unloaded. The divisional service units then had to reach the assembly areas by marching overland. However, since road conditions were poor at this time of the year, snow-clearing detachments had to be provided to keep the Salzburg–Liezen–Bruck and Vienna–Bruck–Graz roads clear. The same roads also had to be used by those divisions that moved solely by motor transportation. Since rigid traffic control was enforced and traffic regulations were strictly adhered to, the execution of these movements did not entail any undue delay.

2. The area around Nagykanizsa was selected for the assembly of the one motorized infantry and two panzer divisions subordinated to XLVI Panzer Corps headquarters. Some of the tracked vehicles moved upon the Vienna–Sopron–Nagykanizsa railroad line, whose feeder capacity was twelve trains a day. Other elements detrained in the Budapest–Szekesfehervar area and continued on to Nagykanizsa by road. Some of the motorized columns moved directly from Vienna by road since the Hungarian highways were clear of snow.

The above-mentioned capacity figures of railroads and highways were eventually reached, but not before many difficulties had been overcome. The main problem was that no preparatory work had been started until the evening of 27 March. The system of classifying all major railroad lines according to their capacity, introduced at the beginning of the war, and the method applied in processing military rail movements both proved efficient during this emergency. The maximum performance schedule, which required the almost complete stoppage of all nonmilitary traffic, had to be resorted to only on the Austrian railroads. Aside from conserving personnel and materiel, the adherence to normal train schedules whenever possible permitted the Germans to camouflage the movements to the assembly areas right up to the time when the first contingents arrived at the detraining points.

Transportation bottlenecks in the Graz area made it necessary to resort to a complicated system of segregating troop shipments. Only vital combat elements could be included in the forward echelon of the infantry divisions. All divisional units that could be temporarily dispensed with, especially the bulk of the supply trains, were either held back for later shipment or sent to detraining points located far to the rear. This was the first time that such a divorcement of combat and service echelons became necessary and was put into effect. During its subsequent application in Russia, this improvised measure was further perfected and proved to be invaluable.

The cooperative attitude of the Hungarian transportation personnel made it possible to increase the capacity of the Nagykanizsa detraining area in record time. The German Movement Control headquarters in Budapest, recently transferred from Bratislava, was responsible for the preparations that had to be completed within three days. All loading ramps in the area had to be enlarged and reinforced to handle heavy loads, new sidings had to be laid, and adequate antiaircraft protection had to be provided. To increase the capacity of the railroads in Hungary and Bulgaria, the Army railroad transportation agencies formed a reserve pool of locomotives and box cars suitable for troop transports.

Special measures also had to be taken to ensure the flow of supplies into the Balkans once the campaign had started. The line Belgrade–Nis–Salonika, the only one capable of handling fully loaded trains, was vitally needed for this purpose. Railroad engineer troops and construction equipment had to be reserved for the immediate restoration of this line after it had fallen into German hands.

The Bulgarian railroads were connected with the Belgrade–Nis–Salonika line. To avoid timeconsuming reloading operations, troop and supply trains destined for Bulgaria were loaded at "Balkan Capacity," which was two-thirds of the normal weight. This necessitated a rearrangement of the loading and unloading schedules, which was accomplished with the cooperation of the Bulgarian General Staff and railroad authorities.

II. The Danube as a Route of Transportation

The Danube was of vital importance to the German war effort. Oil from Romania and agricultural products from the Balkans were shipped to Germany along the great waterway. To switch this traffic to the inadequate rail net was impossible, and any disruption in the river shipping was bound to have a telling effect. With the outbreak of hostilities in Yugoslavia, all Danube shipping would have to be suspended; its resumption would depend on the progress of the

Figure 5. German emergency bridge replaces demolished structure.

military operations as well as on the extent of demolitions and mine obstacles.

At the defile of the Iron Gate, where the Danube forms the boundary between Yugoslavia and Romania, a fairly long stretch of the river is canalized. Because of the numerous locks and dams this portion of the river was considered to be extremely vulnerable. It was known that the Yugoslavs had prepared some acts of sabotage along the Danube and intended to mine the Iron Gate. Therefore, a reinforced German engineer battalion, forming part of the military mission stationed in Romania, was assigned the task of seizing and protecting this vital area.

According to a digest of captured Yugoslav documents that was written by the Foreign and Counterintelligence Office of the Armed Forces High Command after the conclusion of the campaign, there existed a plan for blocking the Iron Gate in order to paralyze German Danube shipping. This plan, said to have been prepared by British agents in April 1940, failed because of German watchfulness. The British allegedly planned to sink cement barges in the Danube shipping channel. Moreover, they were supposed to have organized a network of local agents who were to destroy port facilities and military installations and sabotage German ships while they were in Yugoslav ports.

During the Balkan campaigns the Danube actually did not play a major role as a military route of transportation. The available shipping facilities were barely sufficient for the transportation of essential materials. Although the military transportation agencies had repeatedly pointed to the urgency of a large-scale construction program of Danube vessels, Hitler had refused to allocate the necessary steel for this purpose.

III. Other Logistical Planning

In 1941 the two best railroad lines in the Balkans ran from Belgrade via Nis to Salonika and Sofiya, respectively. The use of these two vital supply arteries was denied to the German Army. Therefore the following precautionary steps had to be taken to ensure the uninterrrupted flow of supplies to the Twelfth Army forces in Bulgaria:

1. Heavy truck transportation units at the disposal of the Army High Command, carrying capacity loads, were transferred to Romania and from there to Bulgaria.

2. A number of barges, loaded with a total of 10,000 tons of supplies, and a tanker were assembling at Vienna destined for Belgrade, where a supply base was to be established as soon as possible.

3. Another river fleet, carrying 16,000 tons of rations and ammunition, was standing by on the Danube between Regensburg and Vienna. The vessels were destined for the German forces in Romania and were to sail down the Danube as soon as the waterway had been reopened to shipping.

Providing Second Army with the necessary supplies presented no particular problems and caused no delay in the launching of the operations. When surgical hospitals failed to arrive, for example, they were replaced by additional hospital trains.

The logistical planning was greatly facilitated by the establishment of a supply base near Vienna during the summer of 1940. Soviet political activities in the Balkans had prompted the Army High Command to stockpile large quantities of supplies at the gateway to southeastern Europe . The existence of this base made it possible to meet the sudden and unexpected demands of the Yugoslav campaign without shifting supplies from the interior of Germany, a step that would have delayed the operation considerably.

IV. The Assembly of Second Army

During the winter of 1940-41, Second Army headquarters in Munich had been responsible for training the divisions stationed in southern Germany and the former Czechoslovak territory. When Second Army headquarters was alerted for the Yugoslav attack, its training mission was assumed by Eleventh Army.

Toward the end of March 1941 no forces other than a few infantry divisions were available in Germany for immediate commitment. Those armored and motorized infantry divisions that happened to be in Germany at the time were in the process of activation, reorganization, or rehabilitation. The mobile divisions needed by Second Army therefore had to be drawn from France and the Russian border, and their transfer to the Balkans could easily have resulted in delays. The only available mountain division, whose employment was essential for the successful conduct of the Yugoslav campaign, had to be brought east from France. Similar difficulties were encountered in assembling the necessary GHQ units and artillery, engineer, and service troops. The following chart shows the problem involved in assembling the divisions assigned to Second Army:

Assembly of Second Army Units

Unit	Stationed in—	Means of transportation
Second Army HQ Staff	Germany	Organic.
8th Panzer Division	France	Railroad and Organic.
14th Panzer Division	Russian border	Railroad and Organic.
16th Motorized Inf. Div.	France	Railroad and Organic.
1st Mountain Division	France	Motor Transportation.
79th Infantry Division	France	Railroad.
101st Light Inf. Div.	Czechoslovakia	Motor Transportation.
125th Infantry Division	Germany	Railroad.
132d Infantry Division	Germany	Railroad.
183d Infantry Division	Germany	Railroad.

The actual movements of these units took place in the following manner: Using organic transportation, Second Army headquarters moved from Munich to Radegund, near Graz, on 2 April. The XLIX Mountain Corps was expected to arrive in its assembly area on 4 April. After its transfer from France to Germany the 1st Mountain Division moved by motor transportation from Landsberg, northeast of Berlin, to Vienna. On 5 April the forward echelon of the division was ordered not to dismount in Vienna as previously planned, but to continue the movement to its assembly area near Klagenfurt, where it was to arrive by the evening of 8 April. However, the bulk of its combat elements did not get to Klagenfurt until 9 April, the eve of D-day, while most of the service troops joined the division piecemeal between 13 and 15 April, well after the start of operations.

Whereas LI Corps headquarters arrived in its assembly area in good time, the divisions under its command encountered many difficulties. The 132d and 183d Infantry Divisions had been ordered to entrain on 2 April. By 6 April about two-thirds of each division had detrained in Graz, and both were completely unloaded by 9 April. Meanwhile, a truck transportation regiment, then located in Paris, was ordered to proceed to Czechoslovakia from where it was to move the 101st Light Infantry Division to its assembly area. Advance elements of this division were to be in line by 9 April. However, icy roads delayed the movement to such an extent that the tail elements did not reach their destination until 15 April.

The efforts made to speed up the concentration of LII Infantry Corps were of little avail. By 11 April, after the attacks were well under way, the Army High Command was still in the dark as to when this corps, including the 79th and 125th Infantry Divisions, might

(Face p. 49)

become operational. Eventually the former division was transferred to XLIX Mountain Corps, while the latter, remaining under the command of LII Corps, was held in reserve. It was 12 April when the first ten trains carrying the 79th Infantry Division pulled into the assembly area.

Only the assembly of XLVI Panzer Corps went according to schedule. The advance echelon of the 16th Motorized Infantry Division arrived in Vienna by rail on 8 April and immediately proceeded from there to the concentration area in Hungary by organic transportation. By the evening of 7 April, the 14th Panzer Division arrived in Nagykanizsa, while the 8th Panzer Division assembled its forces to the north of Lake Balaton. Although the snow had melted, the movements of all three divisions were hampered by heavy rains, and it was necessary to employ additional traffic control elements to avoid undue stoppages. However, when the lead elements of the 16th Motorized Infantry Division arrived in their assembly area on 9 April, the XLVI Panzer Corps was the only major Second Army command whose units were fully prepared to jumpoff on D-day.

Chapter 9

Operations

I. The Air Bombardment of Belgrade

The Luftwaffe opened the assault on Yugoslavia by conducting a saturation-type bombing raid on the capital in the early morning hours of 6 April. (Map 4) Flying in relays from airfields in Austria and Romania, 150 bombers and dive-bombers protected by a heavy fighter escort participated in the attack. The initial raid was carried out at fifteen-minute intervals in three distinct waves, each lasting for approximately twenty minutes. Thus, the city was subjected to a rain of bombs for almost one and a half hours. The German bombardiers directed their main effort against the center of the city, where the principal government buildings were located.

The weak Yugoslav Air Force and the inadequate flak defenses were quickly wiped out by the first wave, permitting the dive-bombers to come down to roof-top levels. Against the loss of but two German fighters, twenty Yugoslav planes were shot down and forty-four were destroyed on the ground. When the attack was over, more than 17,000 inhabitants lay dead under the debris. This devastating blow virtually destroyed all means of communication between the Yugoslav high command and the forces in the field. Although some elements of the general staff managed to escape to one of the suburbs, coordination and control of the military operations in the field were rendered impossible from the outset.

Having thus delivered the knockout blow to the enemy nerve center, the VIII Air Corps was able to devote its maximum effort to such targets of opportunity as Yugoslav airfields, routes of communication, and troop concentrations, and to the close support of German ground operations.

II. The Three-Pronged Drive on the Yugoslav Capital

Three separate ground forces converged on Belgrade from different directions. They were launched as follows:

1. *First Panzer Group (Twelfth Army)*

Early in the morning of 8 April, the First Panzer Group jumped off from its assembly area northwest of Sofiya. Crossing the frontier near Pirot, the XIV Panzer Corps, spearheaded by the 11th Panzer Division, followed by the 5th Panzer, 294th Infantry, and 4th Mountain Divisions, advanced in a northwesterly direction toward Nis. Despite unfavorable weather, numerous road blocks, and tough resistance by the Yugoslav Fifth Army, the 11th Panzer Division, effectively supported by strong artillery and Luftwaffe forces, quickly gained ground and broke through the enemy lines on the first day of the attack. The Yugoslav army commander was so greatly impressed by this initial German success that he ordered his forces to withdraw behind the Morava. This maneuver could not be executed in time because, as early as 9 April, the German lead tanks rumbled into Nis and immediately continued their drive toward Belgrade. From Nis northwestward the terrain became more favorable since the armored columns could follow the Morava valley all the way to the Yugoslav capital.

South of Paracin and southwest of Kragujevac Yugoslav Fifth Army units attempted to stem the tide of the advance but were quickly routed after some heavy fighting. More than 5,000 prisoners were taken in this one encounter.

Meanwhile, the 5th Panzer Division became temporarily stalled along the poor roads near Pirot. After the division got rolling again, it was ordered to turn southward just below Nis and cut off the enemy forces around Leskovac. When it became apparent that the Nis front was about to collapse, the 5th Panzer Division reverted to the direct control of Twelfth Army and joined the XL Panzer Corps for the Greek campaign.

Figure 6. Prime movers towing heavy trucks along muddy road.

On 10 April the XIV Panzer Corps forces were swiftly advancing through the Morava Valley in close pursuit of enemy units retreating toward their capital. On the next day the German spearheads suddenly drove into the southern wing of the withdrawing Yugoslav Sixth Army, which they overran during the early hours of 12 April. By the evening of that day the First Panzer Group tanks stood less than forty miles southeast of Belgrade. The two Yugoslav armies they had encountered were in such a state of confusion that they were no longer able to make any serious attempt to delay the German thrust or cut the German lines of communications that extended over a distance of roughly 125 miles from the point of entry into Yugoslav territory.

2. *XLI Panzer Corps (Independent Force)*

Timed to coincide with the armored thrust of the XIV Panzer Corps from the southeast, the XLI Panzer Corps drive led across the southeastern part of the Banat and toward the Yugoslav capital. This attack was spearheaded by the Motorized Infantry Regiment "Gross Deutschland," closely followed by the 2d SS Motorized Infantry Division. After crossing the frontier north of Vrsac, advance elements entered Pancevo on 11 April. Having meanwhile advanced to within about forty-five miles north of Belgrade, the main body of XLI Panzer Corps met with only isolated resistance on the following day as it raced toward the enemy capital.

3. *XLVI Panzer Corps (Second Army)*

When the Luftwaffe launched its attacks on 6 April, the German Second Army was just beginning to assemble its attack forces along the northern Yugoslav frontier preparatory to its projected jumpoff on 10 April. In an effort to improve their lines of departure, some of the Second Army units took advantage of the interim period by launching limited-objective attacks all along the frontier zone. The troop commanders had to keep their forces in check to prevent major engagements from developing prematurely, which might subsequently have impaired the army's freedom of action and jeopardized the conduct of operations.

The Army High Command was determined to seize intact the principal bridges in the XLVI Panzer Corps zone. Therefore, as early as 1 April, corps elements were ordered to capture the bridge at Barcs and the railroad bridge about ten miles northeast of Koprivnica by a *coup de main*.

By early evening of 6 April, the lack of enemy resistance and the overall situation seemed to indicate that the Yugoslavs would not make a concerted stand along the border and the XLVI Panzer Corps was therefore ordered to establish bridgeheads across the Mura and Drava at Mursko Sredisce, Letenye, Zakany, and Barcs. The few local attacks carried out by the corps sufficed to create dissention in the enemy ranks. There was a high percentage of Croats in the Yugoslav Fourth Army units that were responsible for the defense of this area. Croat soldiers mutinied at several points of the Drava salient, refusing to resist the Germans whom they considered as their liberators from Serbian oppression. When strong German forces crossed the Drava bridge at Barcs on the morning of 10 April and broke out of the previously established bridgeheads, the disintegration of the opposing Yugoslav forces had reached an advanced stage. Supported by strong air forces, the 8th Panzer Division, followed by the 16th Motorized Infantry Division, launched the XLVI Panzer Corps thrust to Belgrade by driving southeastward between the Drava and Sava Rivers. By the evening of 10 April forward elements of the 8th Panzer Division, having met with virtually no resistance, reached Slatina despite poor roads and unfavorable weather. Enemy pockets were quickly mopped up and the division drove on in the direction of the capital via Osijek, where the roads became even worse.

That the plight of the enemy was becoming more and more desperate could be gathered from the following appeal that General Simovic broadcast to his troops:

> All troops must engage the enemy wherever encountered and with every means at their disposal. Don't wait for direct orders from above but act on your own and be guided by your judgment, initiative, and conscience.

On 11 April the 8th Panzer Division reached the Osijek region, while the 16th Motorized Infantry Division farther back was advancing beyond Nasice. Numerous bridge demolitions and poor roads retarded the progress of both divisions, whose mission it was to attack the rear of the Yugoslav forces that faced XIV Panzer Corps, and to establish early contact with the First Panzer Group.

At 0230 on 12 April, the 8th Panzer Division entered Mitrovica after two vital bridges across the Sava had been captured intact. The division continued its thrust with the main body advancing toward Lazarevac, about twenty miles south of Belgrade, which was the designated link-up point with First Panzer Group.

On the afternoon of 12 April, the XLVI Panzer Corps received new orders. According to these, only elements of the 8th Panzer Division were to continue their eastward drive to seize and secure the Sava bridge near the western outskirts of Belgrade. At 1830 the main body of the division turned southeastward and moved in the direction of Valjevo to establish contact with the left wing of First Panzer Group southwest of Belgrade. Simultaneously, the 16th Motorized Infantry Division, which had been trailing behind the 8th Panzer Division, turned southward, crossed the Sava, and advanced toward Zvornik. Thus both divisions were diverted from their original objective, Belgrade, in order to participate in the subsequent drive on Sarajevo.

Meanwhile, both the Second Army and the Army High Command were anxiously awaiting news of the fall of Belgrade. Of the three converging armored forces, XLI Panzer Corps was last reported closest to the capital, having reached Pancevo on the east bank of the Danube about ten miles east of the city. South of Belgrade resistance stiffened as the 11th Panzer Division, spearheading the First Panzer Group forces, neared the capital.

4. *The fall of Belgrade*

Since three separate attack forces were converging on Belgrade simultaneously, the Army High Command was not immediately able to determine which force was the first to reach the enemy capital. Toward early evening of 12 April, SS-Obersturmfuehrer (1st Lt.) Klingenberg of the 2d SS Motorized Infantry Division, finding all Danube bridges destroyed, took an SS patrol across the river in captured pneumatic rafts. The patrol entered the city unmolested, and at 1700 hoisted the Nazi flag atop the German legation. About two hours later the mayor of Belgrade officially handed over the city to Klingenberg who was accompanied by a representative of the German Foreign Ministry, previously interned by the Yugoslavs.

At Second Army headquarters, no word from the 8th Panzer Division elements, which were last reported approaching the western outskirts of Belgrade, had been received for twenty-four hours. Finally, at 1152 on 13 April the following radio message came through from the operations officer of the division:

> During the night the 8th Panzer Division drove into Belgrade, occupied the center of the city, and hoisted the Swastika flag.

However, since better communications had existed between Second Army and First Panzer Group, the following flash was received shortly before the 8th Panzer Division message came in:

> Panzer Group von Kleist has taken Belgrade from the south. Patrols of Motorized Infantry Regiment "Gross Deutschland" have entered the city from the north. With General von Kleist at the head, the 11th Panzer Division has been rolling into the capital since 0632.

Thus the race for Belgrade ended in a close finish with all three forces reaching their objective almost simultaneously. With the fall of the city, the First Panzer Group was transferred from the Twelfth to the Second Army, while the XLVI Panzer Corps was placed under the direct command of the panzer group for the next phase of the operation—the pursuit and final destruction of the remnants of the Yugoslav Army.

III. Secondary Attacks

Before and during the main drive on Belgrade a series of secondary attacks and small unit actions took place across the Austrian-Yugoslav frontier, where the terrain was unsuitable for motorized units. The following actions were of particular significance:

1. *The "Feuerzauber" Probing Attacks*

Under the code designation "Feuerzauber," units composed of cadre personnel and recently inducted trainees were organized into several waves of special assault troops. The elements comprising the first wave consisted of four battalion staffs commanding nine rifle companies, two mountain artillery batteries, one self-propelled medium artillery battery, two mountain engineer platoons, four antitank companies, and three signal and four bicycle platoons. Additional waves were subsequently formed, involving altogether about two-thirds of a mountain training division plus some attached specialist troops.

Originally these units were merely to reinforce the frontier guards and cover the gradually assembling Second Army forces along the southern border of Carinthia and Styria. This purely defensive mission, however, did not satisfy the aggressive commanders of the special assault units. Between 6 and 10 April, they took upon themselves to conduct numerous raids deep into enemy-held territory and to seize and hold many strong points along the border, thereby contributing to the rapid success of the offensive proper.

The first wave of assault units moved south from Graz in the direction of the Yugoslav border on 27 March. One of them, designated "Force Palten" after the captain in command, was assembled near Spielfeld during the first days of April. Its original mission was to secure the frontier and the vital bridge across the Mura near Spielfeld. However, on the evening of 5 April the force started to attack bunkers and enemy-held high ground across the frontier. By the morning of 6 April several hills had been taken, and scouting patrols probing deep into the bunker line south of Spielfeld made contact with the enemy. They determined the enemy's strength and disposition in the outpost area, and then broke contact. Most of the high ground remained in German hands as the enemy failed to counterattack. Then, toward 1600, mountain engineers destroyed isolated enemy bunkers without any preparatory artillery fire.

Figure 7. German patrol returning from a raid across the Yugoslav border.

On 8 April, Captain Palten decided to personally lead a group of his raiders toward Maribor. He undertook this mission against orders from higher headquarters and despite the fact that virtually all bridges along the route of advance had been blown. Since there was hardly any enemy interference, troops and equipment could be ferried across the Pesnica stream on pneumatic rafts. The vehicles had to be left behind, and the men were forced to carry their equipment the rest of the way.

After forming raiding parties on the south bank of the stream, Captain Palten continued to move southward. During the evening he entered Maribor at the head of his force and occupied the town without opposition. Much to their disappointment, the raiders were ordered to withdraw to the Spielfeld area, where they had to sit out the remainder of the Yugoslav campaign performing guard duty at the border. Losses incurred by Force Palten were one killed and two wounded, while they captured more than 100 prisoners and much booty.

2. *LI Corps*

On 6 April the LI Corps crossed the Yugoslav border at Murek and Radkersburg and seized both bridges across the Drava intact. During these probing attacks the 132d Infantry Division occupied the Sejanska stream and the 183d Infantry Division took 300 prisoners. A bicycle detachment of the latter entered Murska Sobota without encountering resistance. Since the Yugoslavs were giving ground all along the line, the corps wanted to exploit the situation. The Second Army, however, felt compelled to order both divisions to hold in place and consolidate their newly won bridgeheads. The two divisions would have to wait until their remaining elements had detrained in the assembly areas.

During the following three days the LI Corps expanded its bridgeheads, the 132d Infantry Division occupying Maribor and the 183d probing beyond Murska Sobota. Air reconnaissance reports indicated that the Yugoslav Seventh Army forces employed in this sector were withdrawing southward along the narrow mountain roads leading to Zagreb. Apparently only a thin security screen had been left in place to maintain contact with the German forces in the bridgeheads.

The Second Army thereupon ordered LI Corps to form flying columns composed of motorized elements and pursue the retreating Yugoslav forces in the direction of Zagreb. On 10 April cold winds and intermittent snowstorms hampered the movements of the advancing Germans, and flood waters interrupted the crossings at Maribor during the day. After regrouping its forces south of the

Drava the LI Corps resumed its advance toward Zagreb at 0600 on 11 April. Plodding through difficult terrain during the afternoon, forward elements reached the southern exit of the mountain range northwest of the city by evening. A bicycle troop of the 183d Division wheeling eastward had, meanwhile, taken Varazdin, where it captured a Serb brigade, including its commanding general.

3. *XLIX Mountain Corps*

On 6 April, while the 1st Mountain Division was still on the approach march, the 538th Frontier Guard Division, stationed along the northwestern part of the Slovenian border, succeeded in seizing important mountain passes, hills, and tunnels in Yugoslav territory. During the night of 9–10 April the combat elements of the 1st Mountain Division, which had detrained only a few hours earlier, began to cross the frontier near Bleiburg. Advancing in the general direction of Celje the division spearheads stood about twelve miles northwest of the town by nightfall. After exhausting marches and some hard fighting the 1st Mountain Division took Celje on 11 April. Emissaries of the newly formed Slovenian Government asked the corps commander for a cease-fire. In anticipation of just such developments, Hitler had previously authorized field commanders to accept the surrender of individual units.

4. *14th Panzer Division (XLVI Panzer Corps)*

Early on the morning of 10 April, with dive-bombers clearing the route of advance, the 14th Panzer Division of XLVI Panzer Corps, split into two armored forces, broke out of the Drava bridgehead and advanced southwestward toward Zagreb, the state capital of Croatia. This attack preceded the XLVI Panzer Corps main attack toward Belgrade and was intended as a diversion.

Although large enemy concentrations had been spotted in front of the division, air reconnaissance revealed that these forces were rapidly withdrawing westward toward Zagreb. Though fierce at first, enemy resistance soon crumbled as German tanks came closer to their objective. However, extremely cold weather and snow-covered roads hampered progress to some degree. By 1930 on 10 April the lead tanks of the 14th Panzer Division reached the outskirts of Zagreb, after having covered a distance of almost 100 miles in one day.

In some instances Croat troops refused to fight, abandoned their weapons, deserted their positions, and either surrendered or simply went home. One German regiment surprised an enemy unit which was still in garrison and not yet fully mobilized. A regimental officers' party just in progress was interrupted only long enough to consummate a quick surrender, whereupon the festivities continued as though nothing unusual had happened.

Figure 8. Man and beast working together to pull vehicles out of the mud.

So rapid was the advance of the division that its radio communications with corps and army were temporarily interrupted. Reconnaissance aircraft had to be dispatched to ascertain its exact location and chart its progress. When the 14th Panzer Division entered Zagreb from the northeast it was welcomed by a wildly cheering pro-German populace. During the drive on the city more than 15,000 prisoners were taken. Among the 300 officers were twenty-two generals, including the commanders of First Army Group and Seventh Army.

On 11 April the newly formed Croatian Government called on its nationals to cease fighting and requested that they be immediately released by the Yugoslav Army. During the evening hours the first LI Corps elements entered Zagreb from the north and relieved the 14th Panzer Division.

IV. Italian and Hungarian Operations

The favorable course of the military events along its front led the German Second Army to offer its assistance to the Italian Second Army assembling along Yugoslavia's western border. On the early morning of 11 April the Germans were informed that the Italian V, VI, and XI Corps would be ready to attack toward 1200. To speed up the Italian advance and consummate the encirclement of the Yugoslav Seventh Army forces in the Ljubljana Basin, the German XLIX Mountain Corps was to conduct the diversionary attacks in the north while 14th Panzer Division forces were to cut the enemy's route of withdrawal. As a preparatory step the German Fourth Air Force attacked Yugoslav columns and troop concentrations in the Ljubljana area. When the Italian forces finally jumped off, they encountered little resistance from the Yugoslavs, who were attempting to withdraw southeastward. A great number of prisoners and much booty were captured as entire divisions surrendered. About 30,000 Yugoslav troops concentrated near Delnice were waiting to surrender to the Italians who were moving southeastward in the direction of the Dalmatian coast.

On 12 April elements of the 14th Panzer Division linked up with the Italians at Vrbovsk. The line Novo Mesto–Slunj–Bihac–Livno was designated as the boundary between the German and Italian Second Armies south of the Sava. Occupation of the territory west of this line was assigned to the Italians. However, for the time being the German units on the extreme right wing of XLIX Mountain Corps were authorized to operate in the Italian zone.

Upon moving its command post to Maribor on 11 April, the German Second Army headquarters received a message from the Hungarian Third Army by which it was notified that Hungarian troops were crossing the Yugoslav frontier north of Osijek and near Subotica. On the next day the Hungarians pursued the retreating Yugoslav First Army and occupied the area between the Danube and Tisza Rivers, meeting virtually no resistance.

V. The Final Drive on Sarajevo

After the collapse of the border defense system and the fall of Belgrade the Yugoslav Army leaders had hoped to withdraw to the mountain redoubt in the interior of Serbia, where they intended to offer prolonged resistance. Fully aware of the Yugoslav intentions, General von Weichs, the Second Army commander, decided to launch and maintain a vigorous pursuit of the enemy forces withdrawing in the general direction of Sarajevo. Speed was now of the essence since the German Army High Command intended to pull out and redeploy as soon as practicable the motorized and armored divisions that had to be refitted for the Russian campaign.

As early as 12 April both the XLIX and LI Corps had closed up and regrouped their forces along the Sava River. Sarajevo, located in the heart of Yugoslavia, was to be the focal point upon which the German forces were to converge. Accordingly, Second Army reorganized its forces into two separate pursuit groups. Under the command of the recently arrived LII Infantry Corps headquarters, the western group consisted of four infantry divisions under the XLIX and LI Corps as well as the 14th Panzer Division, the formation that was to spearhead the drive on Sarajevo from the west. The eastern pursuit force, under the command of the First Panzer Group, was composed of six divisions, with the 8th Panzer Division leading the drive toward Sarajevo from the east. The Fourth Air Force, continuing to operate in support of the ground operations, was ordered to neutralize the anticipated enemy troop concentrations in the Mostar–Sarajevo sector.

On the afternoon of 13 April Second Army moved its command post to Zagreb to facilitate communication with the two pursuit groups and direct the mopping-up phase of the campaign from this central location. The boundary between the German Second and Twelfth Armies was the line extending laterally across Yugoslavia from Sofiya via Prizren up to and along the northern border of Albania.

By the evening of 13 April there was no longer any semblance of enemy resistance in front of XLIX and LI Corps. The main body of the German forces reached the Kupa River and some elements were quickly put across. The 14th Panzer Division, meanwhile, sped southeastward toward Sarajevo. As the division approached its ob-

Figure 9. German Mark III tank advancing through mountain pass protected by flak.

jective, reports began to circulate that open hostilities had broken out between Serbs and Croats in Mostar. German planes were quickly diverted to this area where they blasted Serb troop concentrations for three hours. By 14 April the fighting between the Serb and Croat factions had gained momentum and had spread throughout Dalmatia. On that day the 14th Panzer Division reached Jajce, approximately fifty miles northwest of Sarajevo, while forward elements of the LI Corps, attempting to keep up with the armor, arrived at the Una after strenuous marches and established several bridgeheads across the stream.

In the zone of the eastern group, one armored division combed out the sector south of Belgrade, while two infantry divisions cleared the industrial region in and around Nis. The 8th Panzer Division led the way southwestward toward Sarajevo, closely followed by two motorized infantry divisions which were driving hard toward the heart of Yugoslavia, one via Zvornik, the other from Uzice. Among the vast amount of booty were seventy-five enemy aircraft still intact on the ground. During the operations on 14 and 15 April, prisoners were taken by the thousands. North of Nis the Germans captured 7,000; in and around Uzice, 40,000; around Zvornik 30,000 more; and in Doboj another 6,000.

On 15 April both pursuit groups of Second Army closed in on Sarajevo. As two panzer divisions entered the city simultaneously from west and east, the Yugoslav Second Army, whose headquarters was in Sarajevo, capitulated. Leaving only security detachments in the city to await the arrival of the infantry forces, both divisions continued to race southward in close pursuit of fleeing enemy remnants.

VI. Armistice Negotiations

In view of the hopelessness of the situation, the Yugoslav command decided to ask for an armistice and authorized the commanders of the various army groups and armies to dispatch truce negotiators to the German command post within their respective sectors. However, those from Yugoslav Second and Fifth Armies who asked for separate cease-fire agreements on 14 April were turned back by the German commanders because by that time only the unconditional surrender of the entire Yugoslav Army could be considered as a basis for negotiations.

Late on the evening of 14 April, a representative of the Yugoslav Government approached the First Panzer Group headquarters and asked General von Kleist for an immediate cease-fire. When the Army High Command was advised of this turn of events, it designated the Second Army commander, General von Weichs, to conduct the negotiations in Belgrade.

During the afternoon of the following day von Weichs and his staff arrived in Belgrade and drew up the German conditions for an armistice based on the unconditional surrender of all Yugoslav forces. The next day a Yugoslav emissary arrived in the capital, but it turned out that he did not have sufficient authority to negotiate or sign the surrender. Therefore, a draft of the agreement was handed to him with the request that competent plenipotentiaries be sent to Belgrade without delay in order to avoid unnecessary bloodshed. To expedite matters, a plane was placed at his disposal.

The armistice was concluded and signed on 17 April. General von Weichs signed for the Germans, with the Italian military attaché in Belgrade acting on behalf of his country. The Hungarians were represented by a liaison officer who, however, did not sign the document since Hungary was technically "not at war with Yugoslavia." Foreign Minister Cincar-Marcovic and General Milojko Yankovic signed for the Yugoslavs. The armistice became effective at 1200 on 18 April 1941, just twelve days after the initial German attack was launched.

VII. Losses

The losses sustained by the German attack forces were unexpectedly light. During the twelve days of combat the total casualty figures came to 558 men: 151 were listed as killed, 392 as wounded, and 15 as missing in action. During the XLI Panzer Corps drive on Belgrade, for example, the only officer killed in action fell victim to a civilian sniper's bullet.

The Germans took some 254,000 prisoners, excluding a considerable number of Croat, German, Hungarian, and Bulgarian nationals who had been inducted into the Yugoslav Army and who were quickly released after screening.

Chapter 10

Lessons

I. General

The campaign in Yugoslavia must be considered an improvisation, since it was launched before the attack forces were fully assembled. This fact should be constantly borne in mind when evaluating the experiences gained.

In reviewing the operation the following facts stand out:

1. The tactical principles set forth in German Field Service Regulations proved their worth when properly applied.

2. The employment of motorized divisions in alpine terrain against an inferior defense force was instrumental in achieving speedy success.

3. The German tanks and trucks proved capable of negotiating virtually every type of terrain.

II. Coalition Warfare

During the Yugoslav campaign the German command was confronted by the problems of coalition warfare for the first time. It became obvious from the very start that the German units would have to be the driving spirit and carry the brunt of the fighting during the operations. The participating allied and satellite forces achieved success only when they were under German command.

Both commanders and troops of the Italian Second Army lacked aggressiveness and initiative. Moreover, the Italian command demonstrated little tactical know-how and failed to comprehend German strategic concepts. Its intelligence system was poorly developed and often tended to overestimate enemy strength and capabilities. During the entire campaign the Italians, as well as the Hungarians, displayed great reluctance to attack until the enemy had been soundly beaten and thoroughly disorganized by the Germans.

III. Assembly

The assembly of the Second Army forces, based on the premise that the attack would not be launched until 10 April, proceeded according to schedule. However, with the Twelfth Army's attack starting on 6 April, Second Army was forced to take action while still in the process of assembling. In planning the assembly this development was not anticipated; the sequence in which the forces arrived within their concentration areas was ill-conceived in many instances. To assure a more efficient assembly of forces in a similar situation, the following points should be borne in mind:

1. In establishing the march sequence for any troop movement it is vital that the unit commander concerned be consulted so that the forces necessary for immediate commitment have precedence over the technical support elements.

2. It is imperative that those command echelons directly responsible for the conduct of operations, such as army and corps forward headquarters, together with their signal, reconnaissance, and, especially, engineer units, be the first to arrive in the assembly area.

3. Within a division, the reconnaissance battalion and engineer elements should constitute the lead echelon along with the division command echelon, the signal battalion, and at least one regimental headquarters, including its signal platoon.

IV. Other Organizational and Tactical Improvisations

The Yugoslav campaign must be considered primarily as a series of operations against river lines and in mountainous terrain. In both instances, independent combined-arms teams with missions of seizing key bridges and hills proved effective and successful.

The infantry divisions that had to fight their way through mountainous terrain in northwestern Yugoslavia accomplished their missions relatively well. It would have been advantageous, however, if the divisions had been more familiar with the peculiarities of mountain warfare. Advance detachments played an important role, but were only formed when the need arose, and again disbanded once their specific mission was accomplished.

After the initial penetrations had been achieved, powerful armored wedges exploited the situation by breaking through at various points and swiftly moving deep into the enemy rear. It was here that German motorized equipment surpassed all expectations by covering great distances with lightning speed over primitive, winding roads and through narrow, treacherous mountain passes. Road and weather conditions, especially in the mountains, demanded the careful organization of march columns, and the proper employment of traffic control units. There can be no doubt that it was the rapid thrusts of the mechanized columns across the mountains that broke the back of enemy resistance and spelled the early doom of the Yugoslav Army.

Chapter 11

Conclusions

As during earlier campaigns in World War II, the German superiority in armor and air power led to the quick conclusion of operations. Although the German General Staff planners had been well aware of the deficiencies and weaknesses of the Yugoslav Army, they were greatly surprised that the campaign could be concluded within so short a time.

I. Yugoslav Military Unpreparedness

What were the causes that led to this unexpectedly rapid success? Surely the Yugoslav high command must have expected German armed intervention as an aftermath of the *coup d'état*. For one thing the German Army was not actively engaged in any other theater of operations at that time. Furthermore, the growing concentration of German forces in Bulgaria should have been a clear warning that

Figure 10. Disabled Yugoslav tank.

Hitler had aggressive designs on the Balkans. The campaigns of 1939 and 1940 should also have taught the Yugoslavs that German operations were invariably spearheaded by coordinated efforts of Luftwaffe and panzer units.

The idea of completely stopping a force so vastly superior in men and materiel could of course not have been entertained. However, sufficient resistance could have been mustered to gain time to permit allied forces to come to Yugoslavia's aid. The mountainous terrain in the Balkans gives the defender a certain advantage over a highly mechanized attack force. That Yugoslav defenses should have been better prepared is quite obvious. Some of the artificial obstacles encountered in the German Second Army zone indicated that efforts in that direction had been made, but were either insufficient or came too late.

When the German forces struck, the mobilization and concentration of Yugoslav defense forces had hardly begun. Instead of massing their forces around strategic points and behind natural terrain barriers in an effort to conserve strength and operate along interior lines of communication, the Yugoslav command chose to scatter its forces and spread them along the entire perimeter of the country's frontier. Thus, by attempting to hold everywhere, the Yugoslavs lost everything.

II. Internal Disunity

The lack of fighting spirit among major elements of the Yugoslav Army was equally decisive. Almost from the outset this deficiency became particularly obvious in the Second Army zone. Although it had been common knowledge that considerable tension existed within Yugoslavia, the Germans were surprised to see the inroads that the spirit of revolt had made on the national unity of the country. There can be little doubt that the rift between the Serbs and Croats played a major role in the rapid collapse. Whereas the Serbs vigorously opposed cooperation with Germany, as demonstrated by the uprising on 27 March, the Croat element of the population thought it wiser to compromise with Hitler than to resist in the face of tremendous odds. This feeling was naturally also shared by the Croats in the Army. A number of Croat officers even went to the extreme of committing acts of treason. In one such instance, an air force officer flew from Belgrade to Graz as early as 3 April and handed over to the Germans the highly classified list of airfields where the Yugoslav planes were dispersed. Thus, when the Luftwaffe struck these fields during the initial attack wave, it virtually wiped out what little Yugoslav air power there was.

In the ground fighting, shortly after the Germans attacked, entire Croat units simply threw away their weapons and quit. In some instances, Croat officers led their men in organized attacks against Serb elements that were actively resisting the invaders. On 8 April, Croat troops openly revolted in Vinkovci, the main railroad junction along the vital Belgrade–Zagreb line. They launched a concerted attack against the headquarters of First Army Group and held as prisoners its commander with his entire staff until they were rescued by loyal Serb troops. Such occurrences were not unusual and happened in other sectors as well.

III. German Propaganda

German propaganda efforts naturally took full advantage of this open rift between Serbs and Croats. The constantly repeated official line was that Germany and Italy desired the creation of an independent state of Croatia and that the military operations were being conducted only against the Serbs. However, when Hitler was first told of the open animosity among the various ethnic factions in Yugoslavia, he is said to have remarked: "That is none of our business. If they want to bash each others' heads in, let them go ahead."

IV. Seeds of Unrest

The Germans, however, were soon to discover that, despite the official cessation of hostilities, many areas of Yugoslavia were far from pacified. The lack of resistance encountered during the brief military operations led the Germans to grossly underestimate the true fighting spirit of the Yugoslav people. That they were mistaken was clearly revealed during the ensuing years. The Yugoslavs' will to fight, squashed during the campaign of 1941, soon found outlet in widespread resistance movements. Operating from their sanctuaries in the mountains, Serbs, Croats, Slovenes, and other ethnic groups united their efforts to harass and plague the German and Italian occupation forces.

In a letter Mussolini wrote to Hitler on 29 December 1941, the former stated with reference to Yugoslavia:

> Before next spring every nucleus of insurrection must be wiped out or else we run the risk of having to fight a subsidiary war in the Balkans. The first territory to be pacified is Bosnia, then Serbia and Montenegro. The military operations must be conducted with great determination and must lead to a real and complete disarmament of the population, this being the sole guarantee for avoiding surprise in the future. For this purpose our military forces must cooperate according to a common plan to prevent duplication of effort and achieve the desired result with a minimum of manpower and materiel.

PART THREE
THE GERMAN CAMPAIGN IN GREECE
(Operation MARITA)

Chapter 12
General

I. Political and Military Events (October 1940–April 1941)

For a better understanding of the German campaign in Greece, it is necessary to go back to Italy's attack on that country which started on 28 October 1940. After some initial successes, the invader was stopped by the Greek Army and thrown back to his jumpoff positions. During the second phase of the operation the Greeks opened an offensive on 14 November, drove deep into Albanian territory, and threatened Valona, the principal Italian supply port. During this period the British were unable to provide any immediate assistance. In November their ground forces in the Middle East were fully extended by the British effort to stop the Italian invasion of Egypt. The Royal Air Force operated on a shoestring. But even if long-range bombers had been readily available, they could not have been sent to Greece on short notice because no facilities for servicing and maintaining them existed in that country. Moreover, there were no airfields suitable for modern bombers.

In addition to these military complications there arose a political one. Determined to avoid any action that might lead to German intervention, the Greek government refused to permit the Royal Air Force to survey sites for new airfields north of the line Mount Olympus-Gulf of Arta. (Map 5) Whereas such caution on the part of the Greeks was understandable, it was futile since, as early as 4 November, Hitler had decided to occupy northern Greece to eliminate the British threat to the Romanian oil fields.

The Greek Army held the initiative through the beginning of March 1941, but made only local gains by eliminating enemy salients

Map 5

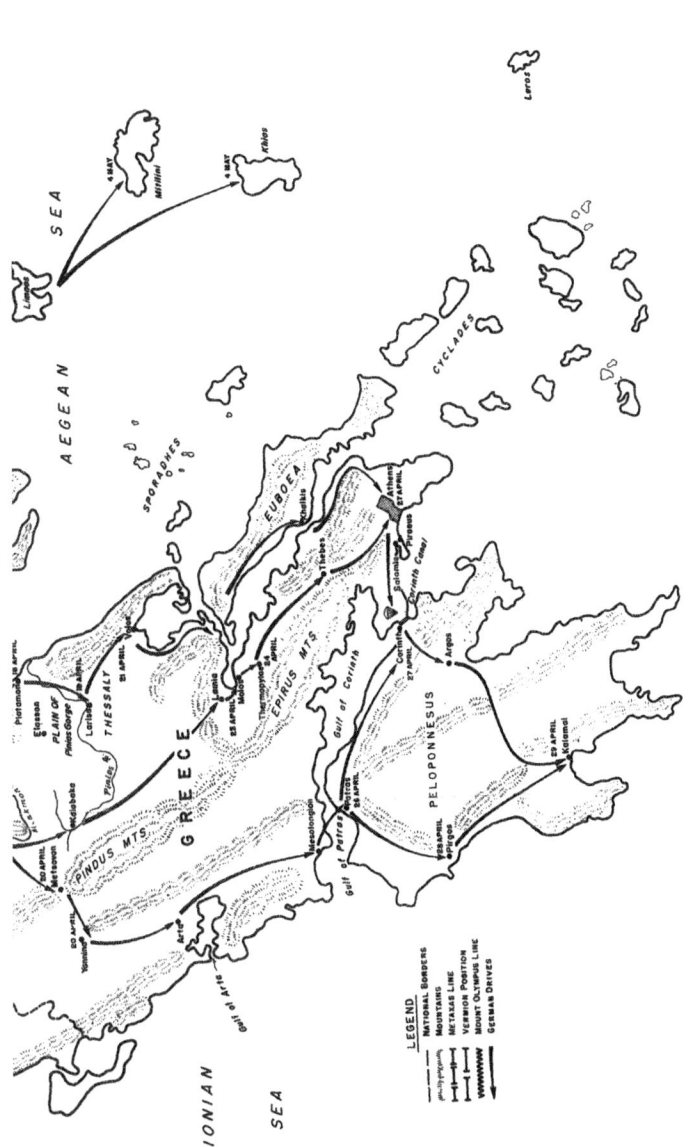

(Face p. 70)

on the Albanian front. The Italian spring offensive, which started on 9 March, made no headway, and the Greeks were able to hold their territorial gains until Germany entered the conflict. Except for some tactical air support received from the British, the Greek Army carried the fight entirely on its own, suffering very heavy casualties.

While the Greeks had thus demonstrated their ability to withstand the assault of the junior Axis partner, a German intervention in the Balkans could easily reverse the situation. In the event of a German attack, Greece was in a very unfavorable position because it lacked the necessary strength to cope with such a formidable opponent. The morale of the Greek forces in Albania was high, but it was difficult to foretell how a German attack would affect them. Moreover, since Greece had practically no armament industry, its equipment and ammunition supplies consisted mainly of stocks that the British had captured from the defeated Italian armies in North Africa.

In order to feed the battle in Albania, the Greek command had been forced to make continuous withdrawals from eastern Macedonia and western Thrace. To reverse this process in anticipation of a German attack was inexpedient because the available forces were inadequate for sustained resistance on both fronts. The Greek command therefore decided to continue its successful resistance in Albania, no matter how the situation might develop under the impact of a German attack across the Bulgarian border.

In this difficult military situation Greece's only hope was that the ground forces offered by the British would arrive in time and that Yugoslavia and Turkey, or Yugoslavia alone, would participate in the struggle against the Axis Powers. If Yugoslavia joined Greece before the Germans were ready to attack, the Albanian pocket could be cleared of Italian forces. This in turn would make available considerable forces to block a German invasion of Greece.

During a meeting of British and Greek military and political leaders which took place in Athens on 13 January, Gen. Alexander Papagos, Commander in Chief of the Greek Army, reviewed the situation and expressed the opinion that Yugoslavia would probably remain neutral. The minimum assistance he asked from Britain was nine divisions with corresponding air support. These divisions should arrive in eastern Macedonia and western Thrace before the Germans moved from Romania to Bulgaria and assembled their forces for the attack on Greece. Secrecy and deception as to the ultimate destination of the British expeditionary force, which was to be assembled in Egypt, were essential to prevent any German interference. However, all the British could offer was two to three divisions and a relatively small number of planes whose arrival would furthermore be delayed by the existing shortage of shipping. They suggested the immediate dispatch of a small token force of less than divisional strength. This offer was rejected by the Greeks who feared that the arrival of such a contingent would precipitate a German attack without giving them any sizable assistance. British help would be requested if and when German troops crossed the Danube from Romania into Bulgaria. Such an overt act would be considered as a preliminary step to an attack on Greece.

The Greek Government apparently informed the Yugoslavs of this decision, and they in turn made it known to the German Government. General Papagos writes on this subject:

> This, incidentally, disposes of the German assertion that they were forced to attack us only in order to expel the British from Greece, for they knew that, if they had not marched into Bulgaria, no British troops would have landed in Greece. Their assertion was merely an excuse on their part to enable them to plead extenuating circumstances in justification of their aggression against a small nation, already entangled in a war against a Great Power. But, irrespective of the presence or absence of British troops in the Balkans, German intervention would have taken place firstly because the Germans had to secure the right flank of the German Army which was to operate against Russia according to the plans already prepared in autumn 1940, and secondly because the possession of the southern part of the Balkan Peninsula commanding the eastern end of the Mediterranean was of great strategic importance for Germany's plan of attacking Great Britain and the line of Imperial communications with the East.*

Throughout the month of February the Greek Government weighed the pros and cons of limited British intervention and a voluntary withdrawal of military forces from the northeastern border of the country. From the military point of view it would have been preferable to evacuate eastern Macedonia and western Thrace because this part of the country could not be defended with fewer than twelve divisions. Since the combined Greek-British defense force for this area would not amount to more than six divisions, it would have been preferable to establish a defense line along the shorter Vermion–Mount Olympus line which offered very favorable natural terrain features. Political considerations, however, made it impossible to take such a step which would have involved the abandonment of Salonika and the entire region east of the Vardar River. Similar reasons stood in the way of a voluntary withdrawal of the Greek forces from Albania, which would have had disastrous results on Greek morale. From their point of view it seemed preferable to the Greeks to run the risk of being stabbed

---

*Alexander Papagos, *The Battle of Greece 1940–1941* (The J. M. Scazikis Alpha Editions, Athens, 1949), p. 317.

Figure 11. Gun emplacements in a Greek mountain position.

in the back by the Germans while holding the Italian front, rather than to be defeated by both enemies simultaneously.

When German troops officially entered Bulgaria during the first four days of March, the British reacted promptly by embarking an expeditionary force in Alexandria. Several squadrons of the Royal Air Force as well as antiaircraft units had been operating in Greece during the previous months. From the British point of view it was not feasible to desert the Greeks now that forces were available after the North African victories. At no time had the British exercised any pressure on the Greeks by requesting them to resist the Germans. On the contrary, Greek leaders had repeatedly expressed their intention to defend themselves against any German invasion, no matter whether they would be assisted by their ally or not. The British fully realized that their prestige would suffer a crushing blow, if the expeditionary force had to be evacuated in another Dunkerque, but even this possibility seemed preferable to leaving Greece to its fate. In a report Mr. Eden and his military advisers sent to London at the beginning of March, they summed up the situation by stating that there was a "reasonable fighting chance" and, with a certain amount of luck, a good opportunity "of perhaps seriously upsetting the German plans." Even so, there can be no doubt that political factors overshadowed military considerations in the British decision to send an expeditionary force to Greece.

No definite decision on the disposition of forces was taken, mainly because of British and Greek hopes that Yugoslavia would join forces against the Axis Powers. When this hope finally and somewhat unexpectedly materialized at the end of March, the three countries failed to establish a unified command. No such initiative was taken, and there was only one meeting of British, Yugoslav, and Greek military representatives on 3 April. During this conference the Yugoslavs promised to block the Strimon Valley in case of a German attack across their territory. Moreover, the Greeks and Yugoslavs agreed to launch a common offensive against the Italians in Albania. By 12 April the Yugoslavs were to concentrate four divisions along the northern border of Albania and provide additional forces in support of a Greek offensive in southern Albania. The course of events demonstrated only too clearly how unrealistic these offensive plans were at a time when both countries should have attempted to coordinate their defense efforts against the German threat.

II. Military Topography

The assembly area of the German attack forces in southwestern Bulgaria was delimited by the rugged mountain range along the Yugoslav–Bulgarian border. In order to enter northern Greece the attacker had to cross the Rhodope Mountains, where only a few passes and river valleys permitted the passage of major military units. Two invasion routes led across the passes west of Kyustendil along the Yugoslav–Bulgarian border and another one through the Strimon Valley in the south. The very steep mountain roads with their numerous turns could not be negotiated by heavy vehicles until German engineer troops had widened them by blasting the rocks. Off the roads only infantry and pack animals could pass through the terrain.

The Greek fortifications along the border had been skillfully adapted to these terrain features and a defense system in depth covered the few available roads. No continuous fortifications had been erected along the Yugoslav–Bulgarian border, but road blocks, demolitions, and extensive mine fields had been prepared at all border points. The Strimon and Nestos Rivers cut across the mountain range along the Greek–Bulgarian frontier; both valleys were well protected by strong fortifications which formed part of the Metaxas Line. This line was a system of concrete pillboxes and field fortifications, which had been constructed along principles similar to those applied in the Maginot Line. General John Metaxas, the Greek Premier who died shortly before the German invasion of his country, had initiated this construction project in the summer of 1936. Its strongest part extended over a distance of 125 miles from the mouth of the Nestos River to the point where the Yugoslav, Bulgarian, and Greek borders meet. The fortresses within this defense system blocked the road that led through the basin of Nevrokop and across the Rupel Gorge to eastern Macedonia. The strength of the Metaxas Line resided not so much in its fortifications proper as in the inaccessibility of the intermediate terrain leading up to the defense positions.

Along the Yugoslav–Greek border there is another mountain range with only two major defiles, one leading from Monastir to Florina, the other along the Vardar River. Aside from these mountain ranges bordering Greece in the north, an aggressor must surmount a number of other alpine and subalpine mountain ranges barring access to the interior of the country. In the west there are the Pindus Mountains stretching from Albania deep into the interior, whereas the Olympus and Thermopylae mountain ranges obstruct the eastern part of the mainland. Finally, the inaccessible Peloponnesus Mountains hamper military operations in the southern provinces of Greece. Troops are subjected to extreme physical hardships by a campaign across Greece because habitations are few, water is in short supply, and the weather is inclement with sudden drops in temperature.

Figure 12. Antitank obstacles along the Metaxas Line.

III. Strategic Factors

According to military doctrine the mountainous terrain of Greece would seem ideally suited for defense. The high ranges of the Rhodope, Epirus, Pindus, and Olympus Mountains offer many possibilities to stop an invader. However, the defender must have sufficient air power, if the many defiles are not to become traps for his ground forces.

Whereas an invader thrusting from Albania can be stopped with relatively small forces in the high Pindus Mountains, the northeastern part of the country is difficult to defend against an attack from the north. Eastern Macedonia and western Thrace are narrow strips of land that can be cut off from the rest of Greece by an advance following the course of the Vardar River. Salonika, the only efficient port in northern Greece, is situated within this vulnerable area. The supply system of the Greek forces fighting in Albania was based on Salonika. The capture of the port would cut their supply lines and isolate them in their exposed positions. Since a voluntary withdrawal of the Greek forces in Albania was not feasible and Salonika was practically indefensible, the Greek and British commands resigned themselves to fighting a delaying action in the northeastern part of the country. The British fully realized the vulnerability of the Greek border defense system; it was bound to collapse in the event of a German thrust between the Strimon and Vardar Rivers. However, they let the Greeks have their way without taking the logical step of moving their forces up to the frontier into the sector west of the Metaxas Line. General Maitland Wilson, the commander of the British expeditionary force, was of the opinion that his forces were too weak to hold such an extended front line. Instead, he established a shorter position some forty miles west of the course of the Vardar. Running along the northern slopes of Olympus and Pieria Mountains and following the eastern slopes of the Vermion Range northward to the Yugoslav frontier, this position extended over approximately seventy miles. There were only four major gaps in this mountain position: one on each side of Mount Olympus, one through the Aliakmon Valley, and one at Edhessa. Almost everywhere else along the so-called Vermion Position the lower forward slopes were steep and rugged, forming a natural obstacle to attacking forces. The two main objectives in establishing this position were to maintain contact with the Greek First Army in Albania and to deny the Germans access to central Greece. The possibility of a rapid disintegration of the Yugoslav Army and a German thrust into the rear of the Vermion Position was not taken into consideration.

Figure 18. Obstacles along the Yugoslav-Greek border.

The German strategy called for the same blitzkrieg tactics that proved so successful during the Yugoslav campaign. Once Salonika had been captured, Athens, with the important port of Piraeus, was to be the principal objective. With this port and the Isthmus of Corinth in German hands, the withdrawal and evacuation of the British and Greek defense forces would be seriously jeopardized. Daring thrusts by mobile elements, strongly supported by tactical air power, would be the key to success.

Chapter 13
The Defense Forces

I. Yugoslav Forces

The Fifth Yugoslav Army was responsible for the defense of the southeastern border in the area between Kriva Palanka and the Greek border. Three divisions were deployed along this part of the Bulgarian–Yugoslav frontier and one division held in reserve in the Skoplje area. At the time of the German attack the Yugoslav troops in this area were not fully mobilized, quite apart from their shortage of modern equipment and weapons. These factors may explain their low combat efficiency at the outbreak of hostilities.

II. Greek Forces

Following the entry of German forces into Bulgaria, most of the Greek troops were evacuated from western Thrace, which was defended by the Evros Brigade, a unit consisting of three border guard battalions, when the Germans launched their attack. Adjacent to this unit, in eastern Macedonia, stood the Nestos Brigade in the area around Xanthi. The Metaxas Line was held by three infantry divisions, the 7th and 14th east of the Strimon, the 18th west of that river. The 19th Motorized Infantry Division was in reserve south of Lake Doiran. Including the fortress garrisons in the Metaxas Line and some border guard companies, the total strength of the Greek forces defending the Bulgarian border was roughly 70,000 men. They were under the command of the Greek Second Army with headquarters in the vicinity of Salonika.

The Greek forces in central Macedonia consisted of the 12th Infantry Division, which held the southern part of the Vermion position, and the 20th Infantry Division in the northern sector up to the Yugoslav border. On 28 March both divisions were brought under the command of General Wilson. The bulk of the Greek forces—First Army with its fourteen divisions—was committed in Albania.

III. British and Imperial Forces

From 7 through 31 March the headquarters of I Australian Corps with corps troops, the 6th Australian and 2d New Zealand Divisions, and the 1st Tank Brigade of the 2d British Armored Division, as well as service troops, disembarked at the ports of Piraeus and Volos. These forces had been assembled near Alexandria, Egypt, and shipped across the Mediterranean at the beginning of March. Immediately upon arrival, the tank brigade moved to the lower Vardar west of Salonika, the New Zealand division took up positions north of Mount Olympus in the bend of the Aliakmon River, and the Australian division blocked the Aliakmon Valley up to the Vermion Range. General Wilson established his headquarters northwest of Larisa. The Royal Air Force continued to operate from airfields in central and southern Greece. There were few planes that could be diverted to this theater in addition to defending Malta, providing air cover for the widely dispersed ground forces fighting in North Africa, and safeguarding the naval convoys across the Mediterranean.

The British forces were almost fully motorized, but their equipment was suitable for desert warfare, not for the steep mountain roads in Greece. There was a shortage of tanks and antiaircraft guns. The lines of communication across the Mediterranean were very vulnerable

Figure 14. German infantry marching through Bulgarian mountains toward the Greek border.

despite the fact that the British Navy dominated the Aegean Sea. All convoys had to pass close to enemy-held islands in the Aegean. The logistical problems were aggravated by the limited availability of shipping and the low capacity of the Greek ports. Only one single-line railroad and one good highway led northward from Piraeus, the principal port of debarkation.

Chapter 14

The Attack Forces

The Twelfth Army under the command of Field Marshal List was charged with the execution of Operation MARITA. This army was composed of the following units (Appendix I):

1. First Panzer Group under the command of Generaloberst (General) Ewald von Kleist. This force was to thrust via Nis to Belgrade, forming one arm of the pincers that was to knock Yugoslavia out of the war. Since it was subordinated to Second Army as early as 13 April, First Panzer Group and its operations will not be discussed in this part of the study.
2. XL Panzer Corps, under General der Panzertruppen (Lieutenant General) Georg Stumme, was composed of the 9th Panzer Division, the reinforced 1st SS Motorized Infantry Regiment, and the 73d Infantry Division. These forces were concentrated in western Bulgaria facing the Yugoslav border.
3. XVIII Mountain Corps, under General der Gebirgstruppen (Lieutenant General) Franz Boehme, consisted of the 2d Panzer Division, 5th and 6th Mountain Divisions, 72d Infantry Division, and the reinforced 125th Infantry Regiment. These troops moved into assembly areas in southern Bulgaria opposite the Greek frontier.
4. XXX Infantry Corps, under General der Artillerie (Lieutenant General) Otto Hartmann, was composed of the 50th and 164th Infantry Divisions.
5. L Infantry Corps, under General der Kavallerie (Lieutenant General) Georg Lindemann and composed of the 46th, 76th, and 198th Infantry Divisions, was detraining in Romania and did not participate in Operation MARITA.
6. 16th Panzer Division was deployed behind the Turkish–Bulgarian border to support the Bulgarian forces in case of a Turkish attack.

Chapter 15

The Plan of Attack

The German plan of attack was based on the premise that, because of the diversion created by the campaign in Albania, the Greeks would lack sufficient manpower to defend their borders with Yugoslavia and Bulgaria. By driving armored wedges through the weakest links in the defense chain, the freedom of maneuver necessary for thrusting deep into enemy territory could be gained more easily than by moving up the armor only after the infantry had forced its way through the mountain valleys and defiles. Once the weak defense system of southern Yugoslavia had been overrun by German armor, the relatively strong Metaxas Line, which obstructed a rapid invasion of Greece from Bulgaria, could be outflanked by highly mobile forces thrusting southward from Yugoslavia. Possession of Monastir and the Vardar Valley leading to Salonika was essential to such an outflanking maneuver.

As a result it was planned that the mobile elements of the XL Panzer Corps would thrust across the Yugoslav border and capture Skoplje, thereby cutting the rail and highway communications between Yugoslavia and Greece. Possession of this strategic point would be decisive for the course of the entire campaign. From Skoplje the bulk of the panzer corps was to pivot southward to Monastir and launch an immediate attack across the Greek border against the enemy positions established on both sides of Florina. Other armored elements were to drive westward and make contact with the Italians along the Albanian border.

The XVIII Mountain Corps was to concentrate its two mountain divisions on the west wing, make a surprise thrust across the Greek border, and force the Rupel Gorge. The 2d Panzer Division was to cross Yugoslav territory, follow the course of the Strimon upstream, turn southward, and drive toward Salonika.

The XXX Infantry Corps was to reach the Aegean coast by the shortest route and attack from the east those fortifications of the Metaxas Line that were situated behind the Nestos.

All three corps were to converge on Salonika. After the capture of that main city, three panzer and two mountain divisions were to be made available for the follow-up thrusts toward Athens and the Peloponnesus. Twelfth Army headquarters was to coordinate the initially divergent thrusts across southern Yugoslavia and through Bulgaria into Greece and, during the second phase of the campaign, drive toward Athens regardless of what happened on the Italian front in Albania. Actually, the Twelfth Army maneuver would constitute the most effective assistance that could be given the Italians.

This plan of operations with far-reaching objectives was obviously influenced by the German experience during the French campaign. It was based on the assumption that Yugoslav resistance in front of the XL Panzer Corps would crumble within a short time under the impact of the German assault. The motorized elements would then continue their drive and, taking advantage of their high degree of mobility, would thrust across the wide gap between the Greek First and Second Armies long before the Greek command had time to regroup its forces. In anticipation of this move the enemy command could either move up the newly arrived British forces or pull back the Greek First Army from Albania and form reserves which could block the German advance from the north. In view of the difficult terrain conditions it seemed doubtful whether this could be achieved with the necessary speed.

Chapter 16

The Assembly—Logistical Problems

The sudden change in the plan of attack for Operation MARITA, which was the direct result of the Yugoslav *coup d'état*, confronted the Twelfth Army with a number of difficult problems. According to Directive No. 25, which was received at army headquarters on the morning of 28 March, Twelfth Army was to regroup its forces in such a manner that a task force consisting almost entirely of mobile units would be available to attack via Nis toward Belgrade. With only nine days left before D-day, every hour became valuable since a new assembly involving considerable troop movements had to be carried out with a minimum of delay. Unusual risks had to be taken to make up for the delays caused by poor roads and bad weather. Instead of waiting for the completion of the assembly, the two attack groups that were to invade Yugoslavia from the east had to use the "flying start" technique. Too much time would have been lost by waiting for the complete arrival of the divisions that were on the approach march from Romania. This race against time became necessary if the Yugoslav Army was to be prevented from completing its general mobilization.

The assembly along the Bulgarian border was complicated by the fact that the infantry and mountain divisions had to march distances up to 400 miles over the worst possible roads to reach their jumpoff positions. During the forced marches, which took place under bad weather conditions, the accommodations of the troops were of the most primitive type. Nevertheless, by the evening of 5 April all attack forces that were to enter southern Yugoslavia and Greece the next morning had moved into their assembly areas and were ready for action.

In order to satisfy the demand for supplies, which was expected to increase with the progress of the Greek campaign, Twelfth Army established mobile supply points close to the Greek border. Essential supplies were loaded on trucks which were organized in convoys, ready to proceed across the mountain passes at short notice. In addition, loaded freighters were standing by in Romanian Black Sea ports. They were to leave for Salonika as soon as that port had fallen into German hands.

The dumps established near the Yugoslav and Greek frontiers held ten days' rations, one basic load of all types of ammunition plus half a basic load of artillery ammunition, and three to five units of consumption of POL (one unit of consumption represented the average quantity of POL consumed per 100 kilometers).

Because of the length of the lines of communications with the zone of interior and the bad road conditions in the Balkans, strict supply economy had to be imposed. The Twelfth Army quartermaster ordered that no ammunition should be left behind in gun positions. Unexpended ammunition was to be returned to the nearest army dump. "Every round is valuable!" was the motto of an order issued by army headquarters on 3 April.

Aside from rations carried by the field kitchens, infantry units were to take along four days' basic rations and one "iron ration," while motorized and armored troops were issued three days' additional special rations. These precautions were by no means exaggerated, since a number of units eventually operated so far ahead of the supply columns that they were forced to consume their iron rations. In several instances spearhead forces had to rely on captured rations and POL supplies to continue their advance.

The initial allowance of POL issued to all units before the start of operations consisted of five units of consumption. Captured gasoline was to be used only after it had been tested against pollution. All captured stocks of gasoline in excess of thirty tons had to be reported to army headquarters. The VIII Air Corps units were to draw their supplies from Army installations.

GERMAN CAMPAIGNS IN THE BALKANS 85

Figure 15. Oxen and horses hitched in tandem to German field kitchen in the mountains of Bulgaria.

Chapter 17

Operations

I. The German Thrust across Southern Yugoslavia

The XL Panzer Corps, which was to attack across southern Yugoslavia, jumped off at 0530 on 6 April, thrusting across the Bulgarian frontier at two points. (Map 5) It met strong opposition from an enemy who seemed determined to stop the invaders. The 9th Panzer Division advancing toward Kumanovo was thus delayed along the mountain roads, and the 73d Infantry Division drive toward Stip was held up near Carevo Selo. However, after several hours of fighting, the enemy nests of resistance were reduced, and the first 600 Yugoslav prisoners were brought in from the front. By the evening of the first day of the offensive, the spearheads of the two divisions had reached the area east of Kumanovo and Kocane. During the night strong elements of the 9th Panzer Division closed up and the next day the remaining heavy vehicles crossed the mountain passes near the border. By the afternoon of 7 April the advance guard of the armored division entered Skoplje, almost sixty miles west of the border.

That same day the flying column attached to the 73d Division reached Veles, while the main body of the division followed at some distance. The reinforced 1st SS Motorized Infantry Regiment, which had been held back, moved up along the 9th Panzer Division route to participate in the assault on the Vardar defense positions.

The continuation of the operation looked hazardous because a force of less than three divisions was to drive deep into enemy territory with both flanks open. The First Panzer Group offensive in the north was not to start until 8 April and no news on the progress of the 2d Panzer Division attack farther to the south was available. Moreover, the possibility of Yugoslav counterattacks against the rear of the panzer corps was not to be excluded. None of these threats materialized.

The Vardar was crossed with surprising ease and the corps thus gained freedom of maneuver. By the evening of 8 April the XL Panzer Corps began its pivoting movement and the advance elements of the SS regiment captured Prilep. The important rail line between Belgrade and Salonika was severed and one of the strategic objectives of the campaign—to isolate Yugoslavia from its allies—was achieved. In addition, the Germans were now in possession of terrain which was favorable for the continuation of the offensive. On the evening of 9 April General Stumme deployed his forces north of Monastir, ready

Figure 16. German artillery firing at Metaxas Line fortifications.

to carry the attack across the Greek border toward Florina. While weak security detachments covered the rear of his corps against a surprise attack from central Yugoslavia, elements of the 9th Panzer Division drove westward to link up with the Italians at the Albanian border.

II. The 2d Panzer Division Drive to Salonika

Entering Yugoslavia from the east on the morning of 6 April, the 2d Panzer Division (XVIII Mountain Corps) advanced westward through the Strimon Valley. It encountered little enemy resistance, but was delayed by demolitions, mine fields, and muddy roads. Nevertheless, the division was able to reach the objective of the day, the town of Strumica. On 7 April a Yugoslav counterattack against the northern flank of the division was repelled after brief fighting. The next day the division forced its way across the mountains and overran the Greek 19th Motorized Infantry Division units stationed south of Lake Doiran. Despite many delays along the narrow mountain roads an armored advance guard dispatched in the direction of Salonika succeeded in entering the city by the morning of 9 April. The seizure of this important objective took place without any fighting.

Figure 17. Metaxas Line defenses near Rupel Gorge.

III. The Struggle across the Metaxas Line

The frontal attack on the Metaxas Line, undertaken by one German infantry and two reinforced mountain divisions of the XVIII Mountain Corps, met with extremely tough resistance from the Greek defenders. After a three-day struggle, during which the Germans massed artillery and divebombers, the Metaxas Line was finally penetrated. The main credit for this achievement must be given to the 6th Mountain Division, which crossed a 7,000-foot snow-covered mountain range and broke through at a point that had been considered inaccessible by the Greeks. The division reached the rail line to Salonika on the evening of 7 April and entered Kherson two days later.

The other XVIII Mountain Corps units advanced step by step under great hardship. Each individual group of fortifications had to be reduced by a combination of frontal and enveloping attacks with strong tactical air support. The 5th Mountain Division together with the reinforced 125th Infantry Regiment penetrated the Strimon defenses on 7 April and, attacking along both banks of the river, cleaned out one bunker after another. After repelling several counterattacks the division reached Neon Petritsi, thus gaining access to the Rupel Gorge from the south. The 125th Infantry Regiment, which was attacking the gorge from the north, suffered such heavy casualties that it had to be withdrawn from further action after it had reached its objective. The 72d Infantry Division, which advanced from Nevrokop across the mountains, was handicapped by a shortage of pack animals, medium artillery, and mountain equipment. Nevertheless, even this division got through the Metaxas Line by the evening of 9 April, when it reached the area northeast of Seres. Some of the fortresses of the line held out for days after the German attack divisions had bypassed them and could not be reduced until heavy guns were brought up.

IV. The Seizure of Western Thrace

The XXX Infantry Corps on the left wing progressed in a satisfactory manner and reached its designated objective. The two infantry divisions also encountered strong resistance during the first days, although both the enemy forces and fortifications were weaker here than west of the Nestos River. On the other hand, the road conditions were worse than anywhere else, often causing delay in the movement of artillery and supplies. By the evening of 8 April the 164th Infantry Division captured Xanthi, while the 50th Infantry Division advanced far beyond Komotini toward the Nestos, which both divisions reached on the next day.

V. Capitulation of the Greek Second Army

The seizure of Salonika by the 2d Panzer Division and the advance of the XVIII Mountain Corps across the Metaxas Line led to the collapse of Greek resistance east of the Vardar River. On 9 April the Greek Second Army capitulated unconditionally. The number of prisoners of war was not established because the Germans released all Greek soldiers after disarming them.

VI. The German Estimate of the Situation on 9 April

In an estimate of the situation dated 9 April, Field Marshal List expressed the opinion that, as a result of the swift advance of the mobile units, his Twelfth Army was in a favorable position for gaining access to central Greece by smashing the enemy buildup behind the Vardar River. It was to be assumed that British strategy called for delaying the German offensive by prolonged resistance at the Aliakmon and Vardar positions. Any premature withdrawal on the part of the British would seriously endanger the exposed Greek main force in Albania. Blocking the gateway to central Greece south of Monastir would surely be the special concern of the defenders, since a break-through at that point would give the German armor an op-

Figure 18. Road block near Greek border.

portunity to envelop the British positions. If that happened, the Greek First Army in Albania would suffer the same fate as the Second Army in Macedonia.

On the basis of this estimate Field Marshal List requested the transfer of the 5th Panzer Division from First Panzer Group to the XL Panzer Corps. This division was no longer needed for the Yugoslav campaign, and List reasoned that its presence would give additional punch to the German thrust through the Monastir gap. For the continuation of the campaign he formed two attack groups, an eastern one under the command of XVIII Mountain Corps consisting of 2d Panzer, 72d Infantry, and 5th and 6th Mountain Divisions, and a western group led by XL Panzer Corps composed of the reinforced 1st SS Motorized Infantry Regiment and 73d Infantry Division, which were subsequently to be joined by the 5th and 9th Panzer Divisions.

VII. The Break-Through to Kozani

By the morning of 10 April the XL Panzer Corps had finished its preparations for the continuation of the offensive. A reconnaissance battalion of the SS regiment that had been sent ahead did not encounter any strong opposition until it reached the area east of Florina. Against all expectations, the enemy had left open the Monastir Gap. The Germans did not hesitate to exploit their advantage and continued the advance in the direction of Kozani.

First contact with British troops was made north of Vevi at 1100 on 10 April. An intercepted radio message indicated that the British command was surprised by the swiftness of the SS regiment's thrust and gave orders for immediate withdrawal from the Vermion Position. The SS troops seized Vevi on 11 April, but were stopped a short distance south of that town, where strong Australian forces held the dominating heights overlooking the pass road. During the next day the SS regiment reconnoitered the enemy positions and at dusk launched a frontal attack against the pass. After heavy fighting the Germans overcame the enemy resistance and broke through the defile.

On 13 April the XL Panzer Corps commander ordered mobile elements of the 9th Panzer Division to pursue the withdrawing British forces to Kozani and cut off their communications with Verroia, situated along the southeastern foothills of the Vermion Range. The SS regiment was given the mission of cutting off the Greek First Army's route of withdrawal from Albania by driving westward and taking possession of the Kastoria area.

Figure 19. Mountain division on the march through northern Greece.

During the early afternoon of 13 April the 33d Panzer Regiment of the 9th Panzer Division entered Ptolemais, a town midway between Vevi and Kozani. The arrival of the German forces was greeted by heavy shelling from the hills south and southeast of the town. German reconnaissance patrols reported that the road bridge situated about 500 yards south of Ptolemais had been blown up by the British and that a ditch filled with water cut across the low ground on both sides of the road. The ditch was six feet wide and three feet deep and had soft shoulders. It constituted a perfect antitank obstacle. The patrols came under heavy fire from artillery, antitank, and machine guns emplaced on the high ground overlooking the road.

The regimental commander sent out two patrols to find a road that bypassed the ditch. Two side roads were discovered, one of which was impassable for armored vehicles since a bridge leading across the river had been demolished and steep dams dominated both banks. The other road bypassing the ditch to the west led through a swamp interspersed with several ditches but seemed passable even though there was no trace of recent vehicular traffic. Most of this road-stretch across the swamp was in plain view of the British.

The regimental commander chose the latter route for his axis of advance because it offered a possibility to envelop the enemy's dominating positions and strike his flank. The approach across the swamp was very difficult and had to be made at a walking pace under intermittent fire from British tanks and antitank guns. As soon as the first German tanks came within striking distance, they opened fire and drove off the enemy vehicles, knocking out two of them.

After having crossed the swamp the German armor deployed. Seven tanks were stuck and followed later. Speed was of the essence if the plan of attack was to succeed and the enemy was to be prevented from withdrawing. This part of the plan was complicated by the difficult terrain which rose abruptly and was broken in places. At the same time the British stepped up their artillery and antitank fire. As dusk was setting in, the German tanks assembled and suddenly emerged on the British flank with all guns ablaze. The British tanks turned about and a violent engagement developed, the result of which could not be accurately gauged because of growing darkness.

Two British self-propelled antitank guns were engaged at less than 200 yards' distance, while trying to escape. They were knocked out and a few supply trucks were captured. Some of the British tanks set up smoke screens to further reduce visibility and thus cover their withdrawal. As darkness covered the battlefield the

Germans observed explosions in the distance and noticed that the enemy artillery fire was decreasing.

The plan to push on to Kozani had to be abandoned because the German tanks had expended almost all their ammunition. Some tanks had no gasoline left, while the rest had only enough for about ten miles. The British had lost their hill positions, abandoning thirty-two tanks and antitank guns as well as a number of trucks. The Germans lost 2 Mark IV, 1 Mark II, and 1 Mark I tanks in the engagement. This was the first and last tank battle that took place during the Greek campaign.

By the morning of 14 April the spearheads of the 9th Panzer Division reached Kozani. That same evening the division established a bridgehead across the Aliakmon River, but an attempt to advance beyond this point was stopped by intense enemy fire. For the next three days the 9th Panzer Division advance was stalled in front of the strongly fortified mountain positions held by the British.

VIII. The Withdrawal of the Greek First Army

The position of the Greek First Army, still fighting in Albania, was seriously jeopardized by the rapid advance of the XL Panzer Corps via Florina and by the British withdrawal to positions behind the Aliakmon. The Greek command therefore had to come to grips with the necessity of withdrawing southward from Albania. However, it was not until 13 April that the first Greek elements began to withdraw toward the Pindus Mountains. On the next day an advance detachment of the 73d Infantry Division encountered Greek troops withdrawing from Albania across the Pindus Mountains into the area west of Kastoria. Heavy fighting took place on that and the following day, especially at Kastoria Pass, where the Germans blocked the Greek withdrawal, which by then extended to the entire Albanian front, with the Italians in hesitant pursuit.

On 19 April the 1st SS Regiment which had meanwhile reached Grevena was ordered to advance southeastward in the direction of Yannina to cut off the Greeks' route of withdrawal to the south and complete their encirclement. This mission was accomplished by 20 April, following a pitched battle in the 5,000 foot high Metsovon Pass in the Pindus Mountains. Realizing the hopelessness of the situation, the Greek commander offered to surrender his army, which then consisted of fourteen divisions. After brief negotiations, which, on strict orders from Hitler, were kept secret from the Italians, the surrender was accepted with honorable terms for the defeated. In recognition of the valor with which the Greek troops had fought,

Figure 20. German infantry "invading" islands in the Aegean Sea.

their officers were permitted to retain their side arms. The soldiers were not treated as prisoners of war and were allowed to go home after the demobilization of their units.

For reasons of prestige Mussolini insisted that the Greeks also surrender to the Italians. Hostilities between the Greeks and Italians continued for two more days, and on 23 April the Greek commander signed a new surrender agreement which included the Italians.

IX. Securing the German Rear Areas

Simultaneous with the main thrust into central Greece the Twelfth Army had to complete the pacification of eastern Macedonia, western Thrace, and the Aegean Islands. Following its capitulation the Greek Second Army was demobilizing in orderly fashion, leaving only isolated hostile forces active in these areas. The northeastern part of Greece was occupied by the XXX Corps, and on 19 April the 50th Infantry Division moved to Salonika, where it was to stay throughout the remainder of the campaign. The 164th Infantry Division was given the task of securing the Aegean coast and occupying the islands. On 16 and 19 April elements of the division captured Thasos and Samothraki, respectively. Limnos was seized on 25 April, and Mitilini and Khios were taken on 4 May. Even though little enemy resistance was met, this operation was not without difficulties for the ground troops. The infantry units were transported in a fleet of small boats requisitioned in various harbors along the Greek coast. Some of the boats had to travel distances of more than sixty miles. Airborne units, together with elements of the 6th Mountain Division, were employed in the seizure of some of the larger Cyclades and Sporadhes Islands.

X. The Fighting Near Mount Olympus

On 13 April General Wilson decided to withdraw all British forces to the Thermopylae line. His decision was based on an agreement with General Papagos according to which the British troops were to evacuate Greece in order to spare that country from unnecessary devastation. The success of the withdrawal depended on the defense of the narrow pass at Platamon situated between the Olympus Mountains and the Aegean. Another delaying position was established across the Pinios Gorge, a defile leading to the Plain of Thessaly and Larisa, upon which all important roads from northern Greece converged.

New Zealand troops were dug in at Platamon with orders to defend the coastal pass until instructed to withdraw. Meanwhile, General Boehme, the XVIII Mountain Corps commander had to wait until the

Figure 21. German tank burns during attack on the ridge near Platamon.

rear elements of his divisions that were lagging behind in the Rhodope Mountains were able to close up. The advance in the direction of the Vardar was resumed as soon as the bulk of the corps had been assembled. After the Vardar crossing had been accomplished on 11 April, the 6th Mountain Division drove in the direction of Edhessa and then turned southward toward Verroia. After capturing that town the division established a bridgehead across the Aliakmon and pushed on to the high ground at the foothills of Mount Olympus. The 2d Panzer Division crossed the Aliakmon near the river bend and entered Katerini on 14 April, three hours after the 9th Panzer Division captured Kozani on the west side of the Vermion Mountains. The 5th Mountain and 72d Infantry Divisions were closing up along the 2d Panzer Division's route of advance.

A ruined castle dominated the ridge across which the coastal pass led to Platamon. During the night of 14–15 April a German motorcycle battalion supported by a tank battalion attacked the ridge but was repelled by the New Zealanders. On the next morning a special sabotage detachment, which was to outflank the Platamon position by sea in one motor and three assault boats and sail up the Pinios River to capture the bridge on the road to Larisa, had to turn back because of heavy swells.

On the morning of 16 April the 2d Panzer Division repeated its assault on the Platamon ridge. This time the Germans employed 100 tanks, two battalions of infantry, twelve 105-mm. and four 150-mm. guns as well as other artillery and technical units. They were opposed by the New Zealand 21st Battalion, four 25-pounders, and one platoon of engineers. The New Zealand commander had been told that the terrain ahead of his positions was entirely unsuitable for tank movement, and that he need expect only infantry attacks.

The German plan of attack called for simultaneous frontal and flank assaults. After a thorough artillery preparation that started at 0900, the flank attack made good progress. The western end of the ridge was seized in hand-to-hand fighting, whereupon the German tanks began to roll up the entire position. The New Zealand battalion withdrew, crossed the Pinios River, and by dusk reached the western exit of the Pinios Gorge, suffering only light casualties.

The German tanks tried to launch a pursuit but were unable to get down the south slope of the ridge. The railway tunnel near the edge of the sea had been blown up and was impassable. One tank company attempted to edge its way along the coast but could not get through. In the end the tanks were towed over the ridge, a very timeconsuming

Figure 22. German tank descending slope toward Pinios River.

process by which only about thirty tanks were made available on the next morning.

The pursuit through the Pinios Gorge made little headway. The walls of the gorge rose steeply on both sides of the river. The railway tracks, along which the lead tanks made slow progress, clung to the narrow north bank of the river, while the road twisted just above the river bed on the southern side of the gorge. The 6th Mountain Division marched across the mountains and emerged at the exit of the Pinios Gorge, only to find the bridges and ferry demolished and the railway track blocked. The tired mountain troops were met by heavy machine gun fire from the south bank of the river. By nightfall the first German tanks crossed the river, but they bogged down in a swamp while trying to bypass a road demolition.

On the morning of 18 April armored infantry crossed the river on floats, while 6th Mountain Division troops worked their way around the New Zealand battalion, which was annihilated. The struggle for the Pinios Gorge was over.

During the fighting in the Mount Olympus area the Germans were unable to move up supplies because of bad roads and traffic congestion. These difficulties were alleviated by airdrops and by shipping ammunition, rations, and gasoline by lighter along the Aegean coast.

On 19 April the first XVIII Mountain Corps troops entered Larisa and took possession of the airfield, where the British had left their supply dumps intact. The seizure of ten truckloads of rations and fuel enabled the spearhead units to continue their drive without letup. The port of Volos, at which the British had re-embarked numerous units during the last few days, fell on 21 April; there, the Germans captured large quantities of diesel and crude oil.

XI. Continuation of the XL Panzer Corps Drive

When it became apparent that the British had decided to offer stronger resistance along the Aliakmon than anywhere else up to that time, General Stumme, the XL Panzer Corps commander, decided to envelop the Aliakmon position from the west while staging holding attacks along the river front. The area around Grevena farther upstream presented a possibility for an enveloping movement. After having forced a crossing at this point, the attacker would enter terrain unfavorable to the movement of heavy vehicles because of the absence of roads and the multitude of ravines. The movement was nevertheless decided upon, since it seemed the only means of breaking the enemy resistance in this area without too much delay.

Figure 23. German tanks get stuck during the crossing of the Pinios River.

On 15 April the 5th Panzer Division, recently assigned to the corps, launched the enveloping movement north of the Aliakmon with the intention of driving southward via Kalabaka toward Lamia. As expected, the division encountered very unfavorable terrain conditions after it had crossed the Aliakmon near Grevena in the face of light resistance. Extraordinary efforts were needed to keep the heavy vehicles moving over cart roads which had been washed out by snow and rain. Not until 19 April did the division emerge from the mountains and was finally able to move at its usual speed. Lamia was seized on the following day against minor enemy resistance. It now became apparent that too much time had been lost in crossing the mountains, since the British rear guards had meanwhile evacuated the Aliakmon and Mount Olympus lines and established themselves along the next delaying position at the Thermopylae Pass.

Before evacuating the Aliakmon position the British forces had repelled all 9th Panzer Division attacks until 17 April, when the first troops of the XVIII Mountain Corps, driving through the Pinios Gorge, entered the Plain of Thessaly, thus threatening to cut the British route of withdrawal through Larisa. During the night of 17–18 April the British succeeded in breaking contact with the German outposts and evacuating their strong positions that had remained intact. Large-scale demolitions slowed down the German pursuit on the ground, but the Luftwaffe was very active, making numerous dive-bomber attacks on the retreating British columns.

As soon as General Stumme realized that the enemy rear guard had withdrawn beyond the immediate reach of his spearheads, he issued orders giving Luftwaffe ground personnel traffic priority along the Kozani–Larisa road, so that the tactical air support units could operate from fields that were closer to the fast-moving mobile forces.

On 19 April the 9th Panzer Division reached the Elasson area, where it was ordered to stop and assemble. Since it was not needed for the continuation of the campaign in southern Greece, the division was designated corps reserve and eventually redeployed to Germany for rehabilitation.

XII. Regrouping of German Forces

As early as 16 April the German command had realized that the British were evacuating their troops aboard ships at Volos and Piraeus. The whole campaign had taken on the characteristics of a pursuit. For the Germans it was now primarily a question of maintaining contact with the retreating British forces and counteracting their evacuation plans. The infantry divisions were withdrawn from action because they lacked mobility. The 2d and 5th Panzer Divi-

Figure 24.—German convoy waiting to cross the Pinios River on a pneumatic boat ferry.

sions, the 1st SS Motorized Infantry Regiment, and the two mountain divisions launched the pursuit of the enemy forces. For days at a time, German flying columns were out of touch with their respective division headquarters. The distance between Larisa and Lamia, for instance, which is sixty-five miles across partly mountainous terrain, was covered in less than three days despite road blocks, demolitions, and a number of minor engagements with British rear guards.

The supply situation was further relieved by the capture of rations and fuel stocks in the Lamia area. Even though regular supply channels failed to function because of traffic congestion and Volos, the only port in central Greece that had a satisfactory capacity, could not be cleared of mines before 27 April, the spearhead divisions were able to leave the Lamia area with an adequate supply of rations and fuel. The ammunition expenditure remained very small.

XIII. The Last British Stand at Thermopylae

To permit the evacuation of the main body of British forces, General Wilson ordered the rear guard to make a last stand at Thermopylae Pass, the gateway to Athens. On the evening of 21 April German air reconnaissance information indicated that the British defense line consisted of light field fortifications, the construction of which did not seem to have progressed beyond the initial stage. Other air reconnaissance reports showed that British troops were being evacuated from Salamis; 20 large and 15 small ships were loading troops in the port of Piraeus, 4 large and 31 small ones at Khalkis. Heavy antiaircraft fire was encountered over the ports of re-embarkation.

By 22 April a flying column of the 5th Panzer Division was attacking the Thermopylae positions that were defended by British infantry supported by well-camouflaged artillery and single tanks. The initial German probing attacks were without success. On the next day a wide enveloping movement was undertaken by 6th Mountain Division troops crossing the difficult terrain west of the British positions. This operation took place simultaneous with another outflanking maneuver performed by a tank-supported motorcycle battalion advancing via Molos. After offering strong resistance along the Molos road, the British troops abandoned the Thermopylae Pass during the night of 24–25 April.

The panzer units launching a pursuit along the road leading across the pass made slow progress because of the steep gradient and a large number of difficult hairpin bends. Occasional landslides hampered the repair of British demolitions. The railway tracks at the top of

Figure 25. German tanks approaching the Thermopylae Pass.

Figure 26. Construction of an emergency bridge near Thermopylae Pass.

the pass were so thoroughly destroyed that repairs were estimated to take three months.

The atrocious road conditions in Greece had taken a heavy toll of German truck tires. Since no tire reserves were on hand, the vehicle attrition rate of the motorized columns rose to 35 percent after only two weeks of hostilities. The Twelfth Army supply officer therefore requested the immediate dispatch of 1,500 tires from higher headquarters.

XIV. The Seizure of the Isthmus of Corinth

An airborne operation against the Isthmus of Corinth was undertaken by two battalions of the German 2d Parachute Regiment, reinforced by one parachute engineer platoon and one parachute medical company. On 25 April more than 400 three-engine transport and tow planes as well as numerous troop and cargo-carrying gliders were transferred from the Plovdiv area in Bulgaria to the former British airfield at Larisa. H-hour for the airdrop over the objective was 0700 on 26 April.

After leaving Larisa according to plan, the heavily loaded, slow planes took two hours for the approach flight, covering the distance at an average speed of approximately 110 miles per hour. The planes flew over the Pindus Mountains and then dropped to about 150 feet altitude above the Gulf of Corinth, heading toward their objective in column formation. They took advantage of the haze that covered the gulf and succeeded in reaching the isthmus without being observed. The pilots pulled up to 400 feet altitude, reduced speed, and dropped their loads above the designated objectives.

The first to land were the gliders, which touched ground on both sides of the isthmus. The parachute troops jumped at the same time and seized the bridge, capturing a large number of British troops.

The primary mission of seizing the bridge intact with a minimum of delay seemed to have been achieved, when an accidental hit by a British antiaircraft shell exploded the demolition charge after German engineers had succeeded in cutting the detonating cord. The bridge blew up and numerous German soldiers were buried under the debris. On the same day engineer troops constructed a temporary span next to the one that had been destroyed so that the traffic between the mainland and the Peloponnesus was interrupted for only a short time.

During the airborne operation one transport plane was forced down by squalls and crashed in the Pindus Mountains, and two gliders were

Figure 27. The airborne operation against the Isthmus of Corinth.

Figure 28. Right: The destruction of the Corinth canal bridge. Top: The canal after the explosion.

wrecked while landing. Several planes suffered minor damages from antiaircraft and machine gun fire.

Had this airborne operation been executed a few days earlier in the form of a vertical envelopment, its success would have been far greater since large numbers of British troops would have been trapped and thus prevented from reaching the ports of embarkation at the southern tip of the Peloponnesus. By the time the isthmus was seized, most of the British had escaped from the Greek mainland.

Figure 29. Motorized column advancing along the railroad tracks from Thebes to Athens.

XV. The German Drive on Athens and Across the Peloponnesus

After abandoning the Thermopylae area the British rear guards withdrew to an improvised switch position south of Thebes, where they erected a last obstacle in front of Athens. The motorcycle battalion of the 2d Panzer Division, which had crossed to the island of Euboea to seize the port of Khalkis and had subsequently returned to the mainland, was given the mission of outflanking the British rear guard. The motorcycle troops encountered only slight resistance, and on the morning of 27 April the first Germans entered the Greek capital. They captured intact large quantities of POL, several thousand tons of ammunition, ten trucks loaded with sugar and ten truckloads of other rations in addition to various other equipment, weapons, and medical supplies.

The airborne seizure of the Isthmus of Corinth had been coordinated with a drive across western Greece launched on 25 April. The 1st SS Motorized Infantry Regiment, assembled at Yannina, thrust along the western foothills of the Pindus Mountains via Arta to Mesolongion and crossed over to the Peloponnesus at Patras in an effort to gain access to the isthmus from the west. Since most motorized vehicles had to be left on the mainland, the advance guard consisting of infantry and support units entrained at Patras and proceeded by railway to Corinth. Upon their arrival at 1730 on 27 April the SS forces learned that the paratroops had already been relieved by Army units advancing from Athens.

The SS units thereupon returned to Patras with orders to envelop the retreating British forces in the Peloponnesus from the west. The movement took place by rail and the first train arrived late on 28 April in Pirgos, where the German troops were welcomed by the mayor.

The erection of a temporary span across the Corinth Canal permitted 5th Panzer Division units to pursue the enemy forces across the Peloponnesus. Driving via Argos to Kalamai they reached the south coast on 29 April, where they were joined by SS troops arriving from Pirgos by rail. The fighting on the Peloponnesus consisted merely of small-scale engagements with isolated groups of British troops who had been unable to make ship in time. In their hasty evacuation that took place mostly at night the British used numerous small ports. On the Peloponnesus some 8,000 British and Yugoslav prisoners were captured and many Italians were liberated from Greek camps. By April 30 the last British troops had either escaped or been taken prisoner and hostilities ceased.

XVI. Losses

The German casualties amounted to approximately 1,100 killed and 4,000 missing and wounded. The British losses totaled 11,840 men, including prisoners of war, out of the 53,051 who formed the expeditionary force at the time of the German attack. The British suffered most of their casualties in the course of the hasty evacuation during which twenty-six ships were sunk by air attacks. In addition, the Germans took some 270,000 Greek and 90,000 Yugoslav prisoners during the Greek campaign.

Chapter 18

Lessons

I. Employment of Armor in Mountainous Terrain

The invasion of Greece was the first operation in which panzer divisions and motorized infantry units were employed in distinctly alpine terrain. Despite the difficulties that were encountered the commitment of armor to spearhead an attack through mountains proved to be sound tactics. The two major successes during the first phase of the campaign—the early seizure of Skoplje and the quick capture of Salonika—could not have been accomplished without armored divisions. The Greek command was paralyzed by the initial upsets, which were caused in some measure by "tank fright" of the rank and file soldier, as had been the case during the French campaign. The speedy capitulation of the Greek Second Army was the direct result of the sudden appearance of German tanks in the vicinity of Salonika.

II. Air Support

Throughout the campaign the Luftwaffe played an important role in supporting the ground forces and proved all the more effective because of the enemy's decided inferiority in the air. During the later stages of the campaign the almost complete absence of hostile aircraft greatly facilitated the task of the German mobile units, which were extremely vulnerable from the air during their passage through the mountain passes and defiles. In general, however, the Germans found that unfavorable atmospheric conditions frequently interfered with tactical air operations in alpine areas.

III. Flying Columns

Flying columns were attached to the mountain divisions because it soon became apparent that in mountainous terrain small motorized

Figure 30. A motorized and a mountain infantry column share road to Athens.

detachments were able to exploit advantages more effectively than the unwieldy units of divisional size. These columns were composed of self-propelled assault guns and motorized infantry and combat engineer elements. The commanders stayed well forward so that they could evaluate terrain obstacles and enemy resistance at first hand. In many instances the division commander found it expedient to take his place in the lead column. He was thus able to take appropriate on-the-spot action, such as changing the march route of the following divisional elements, whenever he ran into insurmountable obstacles.

In an attack on a defensive position the mission of the flying column was to advance through the gaps opened by the mountain troops during the initial penetration and to prevent the defender from rallying his forces and renewing resistance farther to the rear. During the fluid phases of the Greek campaign the carefully selected commanders of the flying columns were repeatedly able to turn the tide of battle in their favor. With complete disregard of what happened along their flanks and in the rear they drove ahead into enemy-held territory. It must not be forgotten that such daring forward thrusts could be executed only because the Greeks—and during the initial phase the Yugoslavs—were on the verge of collapse. Similar tactics rarely proved successful during the Russian campaign.

IV. Mission-Type Orders

Reliance on mission-type orders proved to be especially justified in difficult mountainous terrain. Great latitude of decision had to be granted to the tactical commanders in all echelons because of the frequent interruptions in signal communications. As a rule when orders were received tardily or not at all, these subordinate commanders went ahead on their own initiative and took action within the scope of their general mission.

V. Mountain Training and Equipment

Specially trained and equipped mountain troops proved indispensable in alpine terrain. According to German experience regular infantry divisions should be committed in mountain warfare only after they have been given adequate training and issued special equipment.

VI. Patrol Activities

The Germans found that the British sent out few patrols and never launched any major action during the hours of darkness. In daytime they usually took advantage of the excellent observation offered by their dominating hill positions without sending out patrols. They

Figure 81. Difficult terrain in central Greece.

often let German patrols approach their positions without engaging them. To determine the exact location of their strongholds, the Germans usually directed intensive fire at suspected points in the hope of drawing reaction fire.

VII. Obstacles and Demolitions

The obstacles encountered by the Germans consisted almost exclusively of road and bridge demolitions. The bypassing or bridging of these caused long delays and required a lot of work. Most of the craters along defiles measured up to 100 feet in diameter, having been made by heavy explosive charges. Much more effective obstacles could have been created by blowing hillsides, but the British engineers apparently were short of drilling equipment. Mines were never laid singly, but were emplaced in fields or rows near road blocks.

VIII. Pacification of Enemy Territory

In view of the impending invasion of Russia, the Germans were forced to redeploy their divisions before the Greek forces were completely disarmed and the country was thoroughly pacified. Some of the difficulties encountered during the subsequent years of military occupation stemmed from this neglect on the part of the German authorities.

Chapter 19

Conclusions

The Greek campaign, so basically different from the earlier ones Germany fought in Poland and France, ended in a complete German victory won in record time. Despite British intervention the campaign was over within twenty-four days.

The British did not have the necessary military resources in the Middle East to permit them to carry out simultaneous large-scale operations in North Africa and the Balkans. Moreover, even if they had been able to block the German advance into Greece, they would have been unable to exploit the situation by a counterthrust across the Balkans. It is worth noting that the British planners in Cairo secretly started to work on evacuation plans from Greece at the time when the expeditionary force was being transferred from Egypt to Greece. The ill-fated expedition was considered a hopeless undertaking by those who knew how little help Britain would actually be able to offer to Greece. General Papagos also had strong misgivings

Figure 32. German engineer using mine detector.

about the effectiveness of assistance the British were able to furnish and the soundness of their planning.

The Germans neither expected nor received effective help from their allies and satellites. The Italian forces contributed only to the extent that their presence tied down the Greek First Army in Albania. Bulgarian forces did not participate in the military operations. In accordance with previous arrangements they were subsequently employed for the occupation of parts of northern Greece.

In the political field Hitler felt obligated to respect the prestige and aspirations of his fellow-in-arms, Mussolini. Thus, for example, he forced the Greek First Army commander to repeat the surrender ritual before the Italians, despite the fact that the latter had had no share in the defeat of that army. Moreover, Hitler arranged that Italian troops march in the victory parade in Athens and turned over to Italian authorities the occupation of conquered Greece. During the subsequent years of occupation the act of giving the Italians free reign in Greece nullified whatever good will the Germans had acquired by the immediate release of Greek prisoners of war.

In enumerating the reasons for the quick and complete German victory in Greece, the following factors seem of the greatest significance:

a. Germany's superiority in ground forces and equipment;
b. German supremacy in the air;
c. Inadequacy of the British expeditionary force;
d. The poor condition of the Greek Army and its shortage of modern equipment;
e. Absence of a unified command and lack of cooperation between the British, Greek, and Yugoslav forces;
f. Turkey's strict neutrality; and
g. The early collapse of Yugoslav resistance.

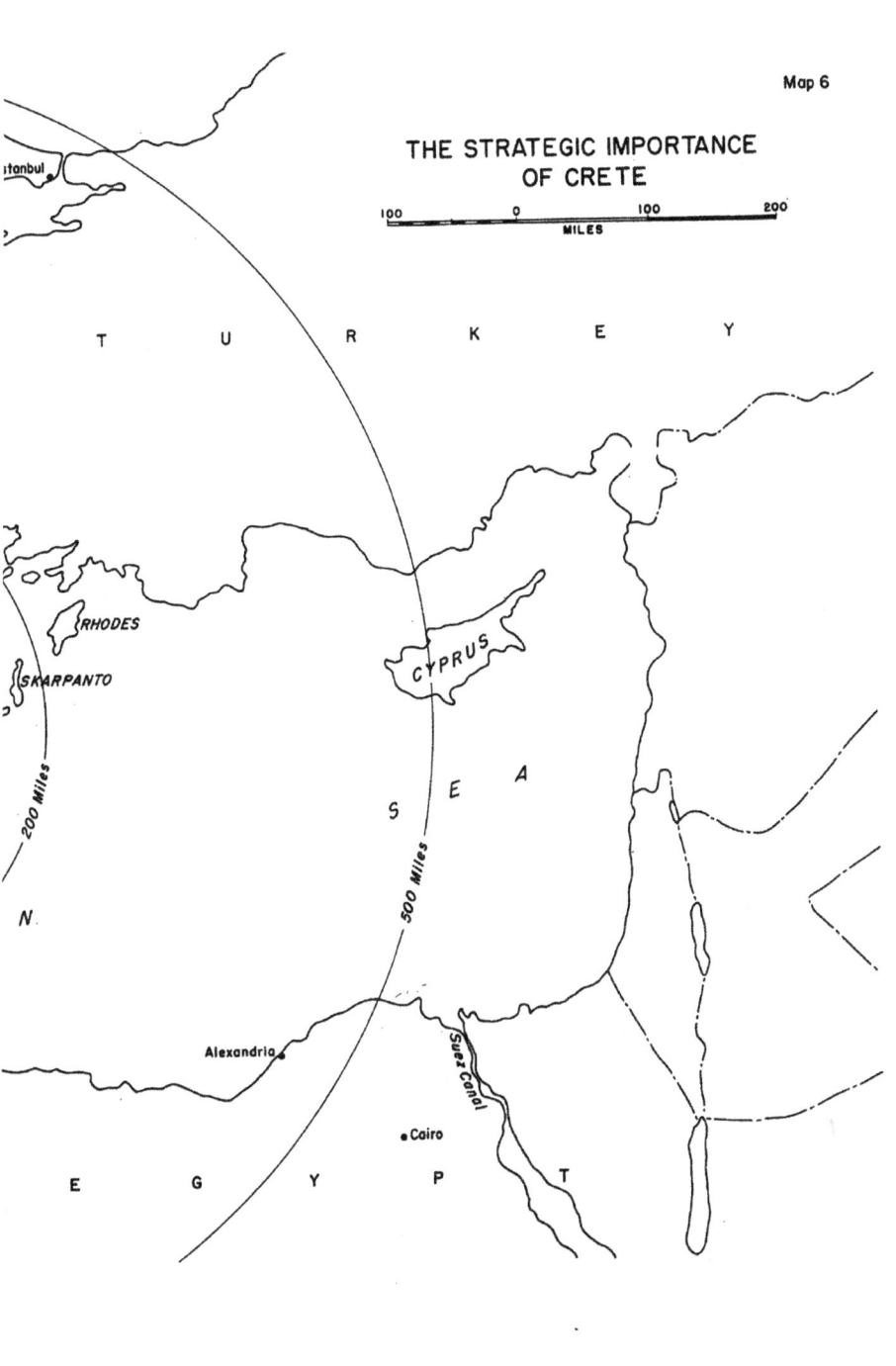

PART FOUR
THE SEIZURE OF CRETE (Operation MERKUR)

Chapter 20
General

The seizure of Crete, effected by the Germans between 20 May and 1 June 1941, constituted the first major military operation that was executed by airborne forces acting independently of regular ground forces. After having achieved local air superiority, the attacker was able to airland a strong ground combat force that eventually defeated the numerically superior garrison defending the island. With his overwhelmingly superior naval forces, the defender intercepted seaborne convoys that attempted to land supporting elements, equipment, and supplies. During the decisive phase of the operation, the attacking air force routed the defender's naval forces, thereby isolating the island garrison. In this trial of strength, air power won a decisive victory over a naval force maneuvering in restricted waters.

Even though some of the conditions that prevailed in Crete may not recur during future airborne operations, many lessons may be learned from the German invasion of that island.

I. Strategic Factors and Planning

Immediately after the Italian surprise attack on Greece in October 1940, the British occupied Crete and garrisoned the island with approximately one brigade in addition to some Greek units. They improved the three local airfields and the harbor installations at Suda Bay, where they established a naval refuelling base. During the German invasion of Greece, Crete was at first the main supply base for British operations in the Balkans and later the collecting point for most of the troops evacuated from Greece.

To the Germans, possession of Crete was of great strategic importance. (Map 6) As long as the British held the island, they were able to maintain naval and air superiority in the eastern Mediterranean; Crete could serve as a springboard for British landings along the Balkan coast; and it was a potential air base from which the Romanian oil fields could be attacked. With Crete in Axis hands, the Greek mainland and the sea lanes across the Aegean would be safe. Quite apart from the boost to Axis morale that the capture of the island was bound to produce, Crete would be an ideal jumpoff base from which Germany could conduct offensive air and naval operations in the eastern Mediterranean and support a ground offensive against Egypt and the Suez Canal.

For these reasons it was not surprising that the German Fourth Air Force, which had been committed in the Balkans under the command of General Loehr, became interested in the seizure of Crete. On 15 April General der Flieger (Lieutenant General) Kurt Student, one of Loehr's subordinates and commander of XI Air Corps, submitted to Goering a plan for capturing Crete. On the same day the Army High Command transmitted to General Jodl a plan for the invasion of Malta that had been under consideration for some time. On 20 April, after a conference with General Student, Hitler decided in favor of invading Crete rather than Malta, and five days later Directive No. 28 was issued under the code designation Operation **MERKUR.**

According to this directive the necessary preparations were to be made to occupy Crete, which was to serve as a base for future air operations against the British in the eastern Mediterranean. Goering was to assume overall command and the XI Air Corps, under the designation of airborne corps, was to execute the operation with the support of the other air force units committed in the Mediterranean theater. The Army was to provide suitable units to reinforce the airborne corps, including an armored combat team that was to be seaborne. Moreover, the Army was to make available the occupation forces which would be needed to relieve the airborne troops once the seizure of the island had been accomplished. The Navy was to be responsible for securing the sea lanes and was to contact the Italian Navy for this purpose as well as for the procurement of the necessary shipping space. Every available means of transportation was to be used to move the airborne corps, including the 22d Division, to its assembly areas, but these movements were not to interfere with the assembly of forces for Operation BARBAROSSA. Finally, antiaircraft units under Twelfth Army jurisdiction were to be employed to provide antiaircraft protection for the German troops in Greece and Crete.

II. Situation in the Eastern Mediterranean

At the time this directive was issued the Axis campaign in the Balkans was drawing to a close. Ample ground forces were available in the southern Balkans, but a major obstacle stood in the path of the seizure of Crete. British naval superiority in the eastern Mediterranean remained uncontested and a seaborne landing in Crete could not be effected until the British fleet had been destroyed or at least driven out of the Aegean. The initial invasion would therefore have to be executed by airborne forces. Almost single-handed, the Luftwaffe would have to neutralize the enemy's air and ground defenses, airland and drop the German assault troops, defeat the British naval forces, and support the ground operations by airlifting supplies.

These tasks were facilitated by the availability of a number of airfields in Greece and on the Italian-held Dodecanese islands, which were at ideal distances for bombing operations. On the other hand, the British air bases in Egypt were too remote to provide adequate protection and logistical support for the forces defending Crete.

Whereas the Luftwaffe envisaged the invasion of Crete with full confidence, the other two services maintained a reserved attitude. Unable to participate in the operation with its own bottoms, the German Navy was all the more skeptical because of the manifest weakness of the Italian Fleet. On the other hand, the German Navy welcomed this opportunity for the possible defeat of the British Mediterranean Fleet. The Army's lack of enthusiasm was based on the assumption that the British would defend to the bitter end this key position in the Aegean since it protected their flank in North Africa and at the Suez Canal. Moreover, there was a very real danger that too high a percentage of first-class troops might be diverted to a secondary theater of war. In view of the impending invasion of Russia, such commitments had to be avoided if at all possible.

III. Military Topography

The island of Crete is approximately 160 miles long and varies in width from 8 to 35 miles. (Map 7) The interior of the island is barren and covered by eroded mountains which, in the western part, rise to an elevation of 8,100 feet. There are few roads and water is scarce. The south coast descends abruptly toward the sea; the only usable port along this part of the coast is the small harbor of Sphakia. There are hardly any north-south communications, and the only road to Sphakia which can be used for motor transportation ends abruptly 1,300 feet above the town. The sole major traffic artery runs close to the north coast and connects Suda Bay with the towns of Maleme, Canea, Retimo, and Heraklion. Possession of the north coast is vital for an invader approaching from Greece, if only because of terrain

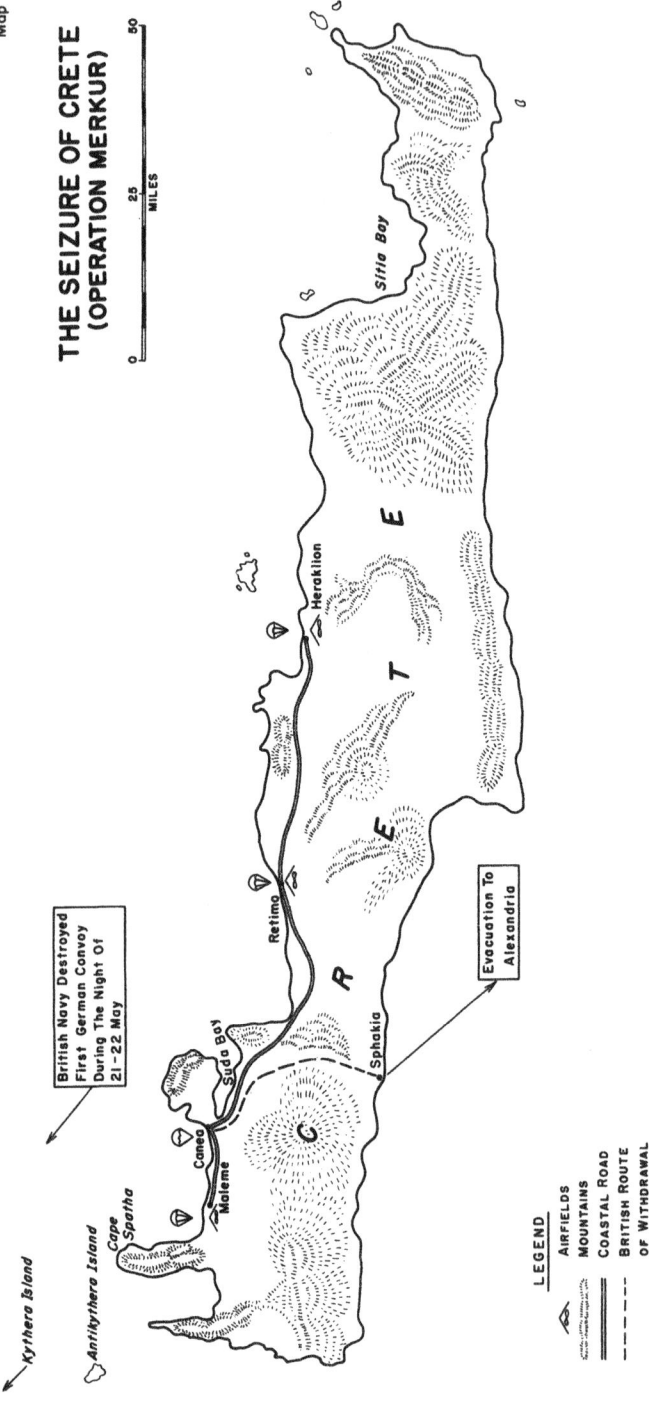

conditions. The British, whose supply bases were situated in Egypt, were greatly handicapped by the fact that the only efficient port was in Suda Bay. The topography of the island therefore favored the invader, particularly since the mountainous terrain left no other alternative to the British but to construct their airfields close to the exposed north coast.

IV. The Defense Forces

At the beginning of the German invasion of Crete, the island garrison consisted of about 27,500 British and Imperial troops and 14,000 Greeks under the command of Gen. Bernard C. Freyberg, the commanding general of the New Zealand division. The original garrison, numbering approximately 5,000 men, was fully equipped, whereas the troops evacuated from Greece were tired, disorganized, and equipped only with the small arms they had saved during the withdrawal. The Cretans offered their assistance to the defenders of their island, even though they had suffered heavily from air raids and most of their young men had been taken prisoner during the Greek campaign. The Greek and Cretan soldiers were mostly inadequately armed recruits. There was a general shortage of heavy equipment, transportation, and supplies. The armor available to the defenders consisted of eight medium and sixteen light tanks and a few personnel carriers, which were divided equally among the four groups formed in the vicinity of the airfields and near Canea. The artillery was composed of some captured Italian guns with a limited supply of ammunition, ten 3.7-inch howitzers, and a few antiaircraft batteries. The construction of fortifications had not been intensified until the Greek campaign had taken a turn for the worse.

General Freyberg disposed his ground forces with a view to preventing airborne landings on the three airfields at Maleme, Retimo, and Heraklion and seaborne landings in Suda Bay and along the adjacent beaches. He divided his forces into four self-supporting groups, the strongest of which was assigned to the defense of the vital Maleme airfield. Lack of transportation made it impossible to organize a mobile reserve force.

During May 1941 the British air strength on Crete never exceeded thirty-six planes, less than half of which were operational. When the German preparatory attacks from the air grew in intensity and the British were unable to operate from their airfields, the latter decided to withdraw their last few planes the day before the invasion began.

The British naval forces defending Crete were based on Suda Bay, where the port installations were under constant German air observation. During the period immediately preceding the invasion intensive air attacks restricted the unloading of supplies to the hours from 2300 to 0330. The British fleet was split into two forces: a light one, consisting of two cruisers and four destroyers, was to intercept a seaborne invader north of Crete and a strong one, composed of two battleships and eight destroyers, was to screen the island against a possible intervention of the Italian fleet northwest of Crete. The only aircraft carrier in the eastern Mediterranean waters was unable to provide fighter cover for the forces at sea or the island defenders because it had suffered heavy fighter losses during the evacuation of Greece.

The British expected an attack on Crete. Their countermeasures were based on the assumption that an airborne invasion could not succeed without the landing of heavy weapons, reinforcements, and supplies by sea. By intercepting these with their Navy, they hoped to be able to decide the issue in their favor.

V. The Attack Forces

General Loehr, the commander of Fourth Air Force, was put in charge of executing Operation MERKUR (For the chain of command, see p. 142). His task force consisted of the following units:

1. VIII Air Corps under the command of General von Richthofen. His forces were composed of 2 medium bomber, 1 dive bomber, 1 single-engine, and 1 twin-engine fighter wings with 150 planes each, as well as 2 reconnaissance groups.
2. XI Air Corps, commanded by General Student, consisted of 10 air transport groups with a total of approximately 600 troop carriers and 100 gliders; one reconnaissance squadron; the reinforced 7th Airborne Division composed of one assault and three parachute regiments; 5th Mountain Division; one regiment of 6th Mountain Division; and several airborne antiaircraft engineer, and medical battalions forming the corps troops. The total strength of the invasion force was approximately 25,000.
3. One bombardment group, which was to lay mines in the Suez Canal area.
4. One naval patrol group and one air-sea rescue squadron. The assistance of additional bombardment groups of X Air Corps based on Sicily had been promised to Fourth Air Force.

The Naval Commander Southeast, Admiral Schuster, had no German naval units under his command. The 63 motor sailers and 7 freighters with 300-ton capacity each, which were to form two convoys, were to be escorted by Italian destroyers and motor torpedo boats. The transport vessels had been captured during the Greek campaign and were assembled at the port of Piraeus. The motor sailers were

Figure 33. German motor sailer three miles southwest of Cape Spatha.

to carry one battalion of the 6th Mountain Division, the service elements and such equipment of 7th Airborne Division which could not be airlifted, and the pack animals and equipment of 5th Mountain Division, as well as rations and ammunition. The cargo vessels were loaded with tanks, antiaircraft and antitank guns, heavy equipment, ammunition, rations, and other supplies.

The sole German Army division trained for air landings, the 22d Division, was unable to participate in the invasion of Crete because it could not be transferred in time from Romania, where it guarded the oil fields near Ploesti. The absence of these specially trained troops was all the more regrettable because the division taking their place, 5th Mountain Division, had no practical experience in airborne operations. Even though the mountain troops gave an excellent account of themselves during the fighting on Crete, their commitment had all the characteristics of a daring improvisation.

VI. The Plan of Attack

Initially, the Luftwaffe had two invasion plans under consideration. The first one, submitted by Fourth Air Force, called for airborne landings in the western part of the island between Maleme and Canea and the subsequent seizure of the remaining territory by an eastward thrust of all airlanded troops. This plan had the advantage of enabling the invader to concentrate his forces within a small area and achieve local air and ground superiority. On the other hand, its execution might lead to extensive mountain fighting during which the enemy would remain in possession of the Heraklion and Retimo airfields in the east. The second plan, submitted by XI Air Corps, envisaged the simultaneous airdrop of parachute troops at seven points, the most important of which were Maleme, Canea, Retimo, and Heraklion. This plan had the advantage of putting the Germans in possession of all strategic points on the island in one fell swoop. A mopping-up operation would do the rest. However, the plan involved great risks because the weak forces dropped at individual points would be dispersed over a wide area and the tactical air units would be unable to lend support at all points at the same time.

The plan of attack which was finally adopted by Goering was a compromise solution. Some 15,000 combat troops were to be airlanded and 7,000 men were to be seaborne. On D-day the 7th Airborne Division was to land in two waves, the first one in the morning at Maleme airfield and near Canea, the second one in the afternoon near the airfields at Retimo and Heraklion. The VIII Air Corps was to provide strong tactical air support during the landings. At H-hour the first groups of gliders, carrying one battalion of assault troops each, were to land at Maleme airfield. The airlanded troops were to neutralize the remaining ground defenses and protect the descent of the parachute troops. Additional groups of gliders were to come in at fifteen-minute intervals and consolidate the gains made by the time of their landings. The combat team that was to land at Maleme was to consist of one regiment of assault troops reinforced by parachute infantry, one battery of parachute antiaircraft artillery, and one parachute medical platoon. A similar procedure was to be followed near Canea, where the gliderborne troops were to land on the beaches. The commander and staff of the 7th Airborne Division were to establish headquarters near Canea.

At H plus 8 hours the second wave was to jump over Retimo and Heraklion without the assistance of gliderborne forces. Each group was to consist of one parachute combat team composed of infantry, antiaircraft artillery, engineers, and medical personnel. The four groups, separated by distances varying between ten and seventy-five miles, were to establish contact at the earliest possible moment. On D plus 1 the mountain troops were to be airlifted to the three airfields, which would meanwhile be cleared of all enemy forces. The naval convoys would land at the same time at Suda Bay and any minor ports that would be open to shipping.

VII. The Assembly—Logistical Problems

The assembly of all units that were to participate in Operation MERKUR took place within a little less than two weeks. In evaluating this performance, it is necessary to remember the poor road and difficult terrain conditions in Greece. The truck transportation available, including nonorganic transport columns provided by Twelfth Army, was very limited, and the situation was aggravated by the fact that supplies had to be hauled from bases in Austria, Romania, and Bulgaria. The Greek railroads could not be repaired in time, and coastal shipping had to carry the main supply load. This task was complicated by the shortage of vessels, the insecurity of convoy routes, and the generally low port capacities. Aviation gasoline was the principal bottleneck because the tanker fleet was too small, and some of the tankers that had formerly been available had been lost during the Balkan campaign. The shortage of gasoline gave rise to all the more anxiety because an adequate supply was essential for an operation in which planes were to play such an important role. In his report of 8 May the Twelfth Army quartermaster stated that traffic congestion, railroad demolitions, makeshift road repairs, and mined harbors in Greece proved more of a hindrance then than during the military operations. The solution of the logistical problems

Figure 34. Mountain troops preparing for airlift to Crete.

caused some delay and resulted in the postponement of D-day from 16 to 20 May.

The dive bombers and single-engine fighters were based on recently constructed airfields on the islands of Milos and Skarpanto as well as in the Peloponnesus. Twin-engined fighters were to fly from Rhodes and other fields within a 200-mile radius of Crete. The bases for long-range bombers and reconnaissance aircraft were in the Athens and Salonika areas as well as in Bulgaria. The troop carriers were to operate from a number of fields near Athens and in southern Greece. On D minus 1 the islands of Kythera and Antikythera were seized to secure the approach routes to Crete, and antiaircraft batteries were hastily installed at both places.

The 7th Airborne Division was moved by rail from Germany to Arad and Craiova in Romania and from there by truck via Sofiya and Salonika to the airfields in southern Greece. The mountain troops had participated in the Greek campaign and were given special training in airborne operations.

These troop and supply movements did not pass unobserved. On the last few nights preceding D-day, the British were able to bomb the assembly areas, but caused little damage. However, the element of surprise—so important in any airborne operation—could not be maintained. British agents in Greece transmitted accurate information on the German build-up and left little doubt as to the next German objective.

Chapter 21

Operations

I. The Initial Airborne Landings (20 May 1941)

Early on the morning of 20 May waves of dive bombers and low-flying fighter planes subjected the Maleme, Canea, and Suda Bay areas to the heaviest bombing and strafing attacks hitherto experienced by the seasoned troops manning the defenses. Most of the antiaircraft guns were put out of action and the defenders were forced to seek shelter. Bombs were dropped at the approaches to the airfields to put the telephone lines out of order.

At 0800 the first gliders, each carrying twelve men, landed near the airfield and on the beaches near Canea. At the same time approximately 2,000 parachutists jumped in waves of 200 each at fifteen-minute intervals. Two of every three parachutes in each wave carried containers with weapons and supplies. At Maleme, the parachute troops jumped into strong enemy fire from infantry weapons, emplaced in positions built into the hills south of the airfield. Many of the paratroopers were killed during the descent or shortly after landing. Because of the concentrated enemy fire most of the men were unable to recover the weapons containers and had to rely on the pistol, four hand grenades, and large knife they carried. One battalion of the assault regiment landed too far to the east among olive groves and vineyards near Maleme and was greeted by murderous machine gun and heavy weapons fire. Casualties were very heavy, and the medical platoon that had set up a first aid station in a farm house was overwhelmed by the constant influx of seriously wounded men. The gliders would have been completely destroyed by enemy fire, had they not been covered by clouds of dust which formed as soon as they touched ground.

The commander of the 7th Airborne Division, Generalleutnant (Major General) Wilhelm Suessmann was killed during the approach flight, while Generalmajor (Brigadier General) Eugen Meindl, who was in command of the Maleme group, was critically wounded shortly after landing. Both the Maleme and Canea groups were therefore without their commanders.

The success of the Maleme operation depended on the quick capture of the airfield so that reinforcements could be landed without delay. To achieve this the British forces had to be dislodged from Hill 107 which dominated the airfield and the surrounding terrain. The remnants of the initial force launched simultaneous attacks on the hill and the airfield at 1500. Despite heavy opposition and a devastating fire from the British antiaircraft guns emplaced near the airfield, the attackers captured the northern and northwestern edge of the airfield and advanced up the northern slope of Hill 107. Suddenly the attackers heard the noise of motors and saw two British tanks charging across the airfield into their rear. Firing all their weapons, the tanks spread terror among the Germans, until the latter were able to move up two antitank guns whose fire neutralized the British tanks. Throughout this episode British artillery and machine gun fire continued with undiminished intensity. Two German transport planes tried to land on the airfield toward evening but machine gun fire prevented them from doing so.

The Canea group, which was to capture the village of Suda and the town of Canea and eliminate the British command staff located in that area, landed on rocky ground and suffered many jump casualties. The few men who were not wounded attempted to gather weapons and ammunition and establish contact with their comrades. Here the German paratroopers were opposed by New Zealanders who engaged

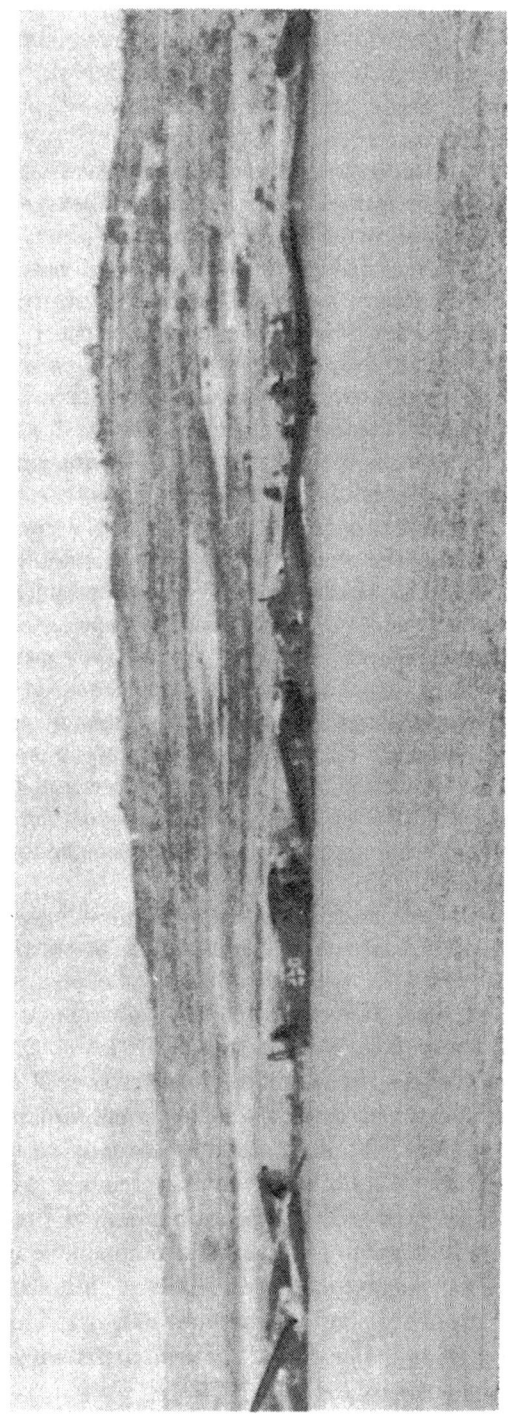

Figure 35. Maleme Airfield with Hill 107 in background.

them with small arms and heavy weapons fire from olive groves offering perfect camouflage for snipers and machine gun positions. The isolated German elements made little headway against the well-entrenched enemy forces.

Meanwhile, the German command in Greece assumed that the operation was progressing according to plan because all troop carriers with the exception of seven returned to their bases. On this assumption, which was proved erroneous only after several hours had passed, the troop carriers were readied for the afternoon landings at Heraklion and Retimo. Because of a delay in the refueling, these planes arrived too late over the designated drop points and the paratroops were therefore without direct fighter and bomber support. One parachute combat team in regimental strength jumped over each of the two points between 1500 and 1630. Running into very heavy British fire, the parachutists suffered even more casualties than at Maleme and failed to capture the airfields, towns, or ports. Some of the troops landed at the wrong points because the troop carriers had difficulty in orienting themselves. After they touched ground the Germans found themselves in an almost hopeless situation. Surrounded by greatly superior enemy forces, they struggled for survival. Their signal equipment had been smashed during the airdrop and they were therefore unable to establish contact with the nearest friendly forces. Although they were completely on their own and faced by an uncertain fate, they were determined to hold out to the end in the vicinity of the two airfields so that they would tie down the enemy forces and thus assist their comrades in the western part of the island.

Air reconnaissance and radio messages had meanwhile rectified the erroneous picture of the first landings in western Crete. By the evening of 20 May not a single airfield was securely held by the Germans. The most favorable reports came from Maleme, where the defenders were falling back from Hill 107 and their perimeter defenses around the airfield which, however, was still under British artillery fire. Moreover, parts of the field were obstructed by crashed aircraft and gliders. Thus, no field was available for the airborne landing of the 5th Mountain Division which was scheduled for the next day. Canea was still in enemy hands and the isolated troops landed at the four drop points had so far been unable to form airheads, let alone establish contact among themselves. While the attacker had run into unexpectedly strong resistance and had failed to reach the objective of the day, the defender was surprised by the fury and strength of the onslaught.

II. The Seaborne Invasion (20–22 May)

During the night of 20–21 May a British light naval force broke through the German aerial blockade and searched the waters north of Crete. Admiral Schuster thereupon decided to call back to Milos the first naval convoy, which was approaching Crete under escort of an Italian destroyer. At dawn on 21 May German planes sighted the British ships and subjected them to heavy air attacks. One destroyer was sunk and two cruisers damaged. At 0900 the waters north of Crete were cleared of enemy ships and the convoy was ordered to continue its voyage in the direction of Maleme. During the day German dive bombers based on Skarpanto and Italian planes flying from Rhodes scored several hits on British ships returning to Crete waters, thereby preventing them from intercepting the Axis convoy. The German troops on the island were anxiously awaiting the arrival of artillery, antitank guns, and supplies, but poor weather conditions so delayed the convoy that it could not reach the island before darkness.

When it finally came around Cape Spatha at 2300, the convoy was suddenly confronted by a British naval task force which was on the way to Suda Bay to land reinforcements and supplies. The British immobilized the Italian escort vessel and sank most of the motor sailers and freighters. Many German soldiers, most of them mountain troops, were drowned. The majority of the shipwrecked, however, were picked up by sea rescue planes. The second convoy, which had meanwhile reached Milos, was recalled to Piraeus to save it from a similar fate. No further seaborne landings were attempted until the fate of Crete had been decided.

On the morning of 22 May, VIII Air Corps started an all-out attack on the British fleet, which was forced to withdraw from the Aegean after suffering heavy losses. The battle between the Luftwaffe and the British Navy ended in the victory of German air power, which from then on dominated the air and waters north of Crete.

III. The Continuation of the Struggle (21 May–1 June)

On the morning of 21 May a few planes were able to make crash landings on the beaches near Maleme and bring in badly needed weapons and ammunition to the assault troops in that area. Enemy artillery fire interdicted any landing on the airfield proper. It was therefore decided to drop additional parachute troops behind the enemy positions dominating the airfield.

Oberst (Colonel) Bernhard Ramcke—who later served under Rommel in North Africa and defended Brest after the Normandy inva-

Figure 36. Airborne landings west of Maleme.

sion—assembled 550 paratroopers who had been left behind on the first day and formed a reserve battalion. He was ordered to jump west of Maleme airfield and assist in clearing the British positions in its vicinity. Mountain infantrymen already seated in their transport planes were hastily unloaded and immediately replaced by Ramcke's men. In the early afternoon four companies of parachute troops jumped from low altitudes above the vineyards near Maleme. The two that were supposed to land behind the enemy lines descended directly into well-camouflaged enemy positions and were almost completely wiped out. The other two joined the assault troops which, by 1700, succeeded in dislodging the enemy infantry from the town of Maleme and the hills surrounding the airfield. The airdrop was effectively supported by tactical air force attacks on enemy defenses. Throughout this fighting, however, the dive bombers were unable to silence the British artillery pieces which were particularly well camouflaged and which, in order not to uncover their position, held their fire whenever German planes were in sight.

Troop carriers with the 5th Mountain Division troops began to land at Maleme airfield at 1600, even though the field was still under intermittent artillery and machine gun fire. Low-flying planes kept the defenders' fire to a minimum and the landings proceeded without major losses. A captured British tank was used as prime mover to clear the airfield of burned-out and damaged planes. As soon as the landing strip was cleared, planes came in and left without interruption.

From that point on reinforcements and supplies kept pouring in and the fate of Crete was sealed. Little by little the entire 5th Mountain Division was flown in. Even more important to the attack forces were the artillery pieces, antitank guns, and supplies of all types, which had been missing during the initial stage of the invasion and which were now being airlifted into Maleme.

On 22 May Generalmajor (Brigadier General) Julius Ringel, the commander of the 5th Mountain Division, assumed command of all the German forces in the Maleme airhead. His first task was to establish contact with the Canea forces and to clear the western part of the island of enemy troops. For this purpose his mountain troops used the same tactics they had employed so successfully at Mount Olympus and Thermopylae. By climbing along paths that were not even real trails and over heights previously considered to be unscalable, the mountain troops, loaded with everything they needed to fight and supply themselves, broke their own ground as they advanced and then attacked the enemy in the flank or rear at points where he ex-

Figure 37. Disabled British tank near Canea.

pected them the least. They had no mules and were therefore forced to handcarry their heavy weapons and ammunition across the rugged terrain. Throughout the struggle for Crete they adhered to the motto that sweat saves blood. In their heavy uniforms the mountain soldiers withstood days of scorching heat with temperatures rising up to 130° F. and nights when the mountain air at altitudes ranging up to 7,000 feet was so cold that they were unable to sleep.

On D plus 5 the mountain troops outflanked the British positions east of Maleme, and on the next day they entered Canea, the capital of Crete, and occupied Suda Bay after a forced march across the mountains. During this fighting the British offered strong resistance and showed no signs of willingness to give in. They made very skillful use of the terrain and delayed the German advance by sniper and machine gun fire. Some of their positions were protected by wire and mine fields. Armed bands of Cretans fought fiercely in the mountains, using great cunning and committing acts of cruelty such as mutilating dead and wounded German soldiers.

The air-ground coordination of the attackers occasionally failed to function during these days. At 1310 on 26 May, for instance, Dornier planes subjected elements of the 85th Mountain Regiment to a heavy bombardment, although the latter had laid out Swastika flags and fired white flares. The air attack continued until 1400 and had a very detrimental effect on the ground troops' morale.

While the struggle for western Crete was raging, German reconnaissance planes reported that a few British planes had returned to Heraklion airfield on 23 May and that reinforcements were arriving by sea in the eastern part of the island. If complete air superiority over Crete was to be maintained by the Luftwaffe, the return of British planes *en masse* had to be prevented by all means. It was therefore decided to reinforce the German troops in the Heraklion pocket by dropping hastily assembled parachute units. They were to take possession of the airfield and, until relieved by approaching ground forces, prevent the landing of British planes. Four companies of parachute troops were formed at Maleme and dropped in the vicinity of the Heraklion pocket west of the town. Immediately after landing on 28 May, the parachute units contacted the embattled pocket force and launched a concerted attack against the British positions, eliminating several enemy strongholds with the support of dive bombers. After regrouping his forces during the night the German commander at Heraklion set out to capture the town and the airfield early on the next morning. At daybreak the German troops closed in on the British positions. Not a shot was

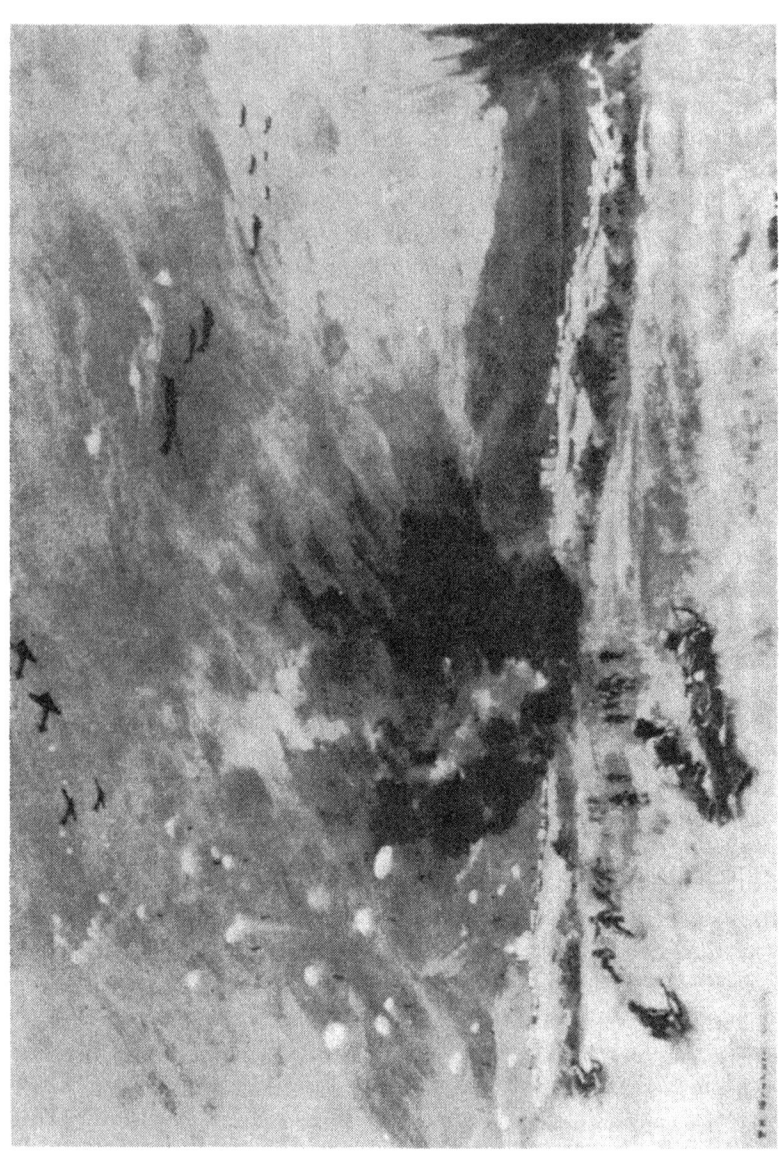

Figure 38. The struggle for Heraklion Airfield.

fired. British naval vessels had evacuated the Heraklion garrison during the preceding night.

By that time British resistance had crumbled everywhere. German supplies and equipment were landed at Suda Bay without interference from enemy naval or air units. On 29 May motorized reconnaissance elements, advancing through enemy-held territory, established contact with the German forces in the Retimo pocket and reached Heraklion the next day. A small Italian force that had landed at Sitia Bay on the eastern tip of the island on 28 May, linked up with a German advance detachment two days later.

On 28 May General Freyberg had ordered the bulk of the British ground forces to fight their way back to the south coast of Crete so that they could be evacuated to Egypt. Since this plan was not immediately recognized by the German command, only a weak force consisting of a reinforced mountain battalion was committed to launch a pursuit in the direction of Sphakia, while the main body of German troops continued its eastward thrust. It was not until 31 May that additional forces were diverted to the south to drive toward Sphakia.

After repeated encounters with enemy rear guards, the German forces reached the south coast of the island on 1 June. The struggle for Crete was thereby terminated. Despite the long delay in the issuance of evacuation orders, the British Navy was able to embark approximately 14,800 men and return them to Egypt. Subjected to severe losses and constant harassment by German planes, the Navy performed the evacuation during four nights.

IV. Casualties and Losses

The figures for German casualties suffered in the Crete operations remain a matter of conjecture. Whereas German after action reports give total losses varying between 3,986 and 6,453 men, Winston S. Churchill states that more than 4,000 graves have been counted in the area of Maleme and Suda Bay and another thousand at Retimo and Heraklion.* In Churchill's opinion the Germans must have suffered well over 15,000 casualties in killed and wounded. Part of the difference may be explained by the fact that the British estimated the number of men drowned in the sinking of the first convoy at 2,500 men. Actually, only two battalions had been embarked on vessels in that convoy and the air-sea rescue squadron apparently rescued most of the shipwrecked. In a recent study on German losses in Crete,

---

*Winston S. Churchill, *The Grand Alliance* (Houghton Mifflin Company, Boston, 1950), p. 301.

Figure 39. The first mules have arrived in Crete.

British military historians seem inclined to accept the highest German figures as correct.*

Some 350 German planes, more than half of them troop carriers, were lost or damaged.

The British were able to evacuate 14,800 out of a garrison of 27,500 men. Left behind were also the 14,000 Greek troops, either dead or captured. The Royal Navy suffered nearly 2,000 casualties and crippling losses which resulted in its withdrawal from the Aegean.

Chapter 22

Lessons

In view of the particular circumstances that surrounded the German seizure of Crete, its success should not be taken as proof for the contention that the airborne invasion of an island is the ideal solution in any similar situation. Comparisons with other theaters of war, for instance the British Isles, are misleading. The invasion of Crete was in a category by itself, but a number of lessons with general validity for similar operations can be learned from the German experience. In general, the success of an airborne operation against an island will depend on the following factors:

a. Control of the air above the island is essential for the successful execution of airborne landings. During the Crete operation the British had practically no aircraft based on the island and were unable to improvise effective air cover from North Africa because of the long distance between the air bases in Egypt and the fields on Crete.

b. Control of the sea around an island is next in importance. The invader's navy must be able to provide full protection for the convoys that have to bring up tanks, heavy weapons, and supplies of all types. During the attack on Crete, British naval units cut off German seaborne transportation and thereby delayed the progress of the ground offensive, which in turn enabled the British to evacuate considerable forces to Egypt. German reinforcements, supplies, and—above all—tanks, artillery, and antitank guns could not be brought to the island by sea when they were most needed. The warning given by the German Navy before the start of Operation MERKUR—not to send naval convoys to Crete before the waters around the island had been cleared of the enemy—had been justified.

---
*German Casualties, Crete 1941, Enemy Documents Section, Historical Branch, Cabinet Office, April 1952.

c. The command channels regulating interservice cooperation must be clearly defined and unity of command over both airborne and seaborne forces must be firmly established. During the invasion of Crete, the German command organization was unified, and for the first time an air force general was in overall command of air, ground, and naval forces. General Loehr, the commander of Fourth Air Force, set up his headquarters at Athens in close proximity to Twelfth Army and Navy Group South headquarters, which were instructed to give him all the support he needed. The command structure for Operation **MERKUR** was as follows:

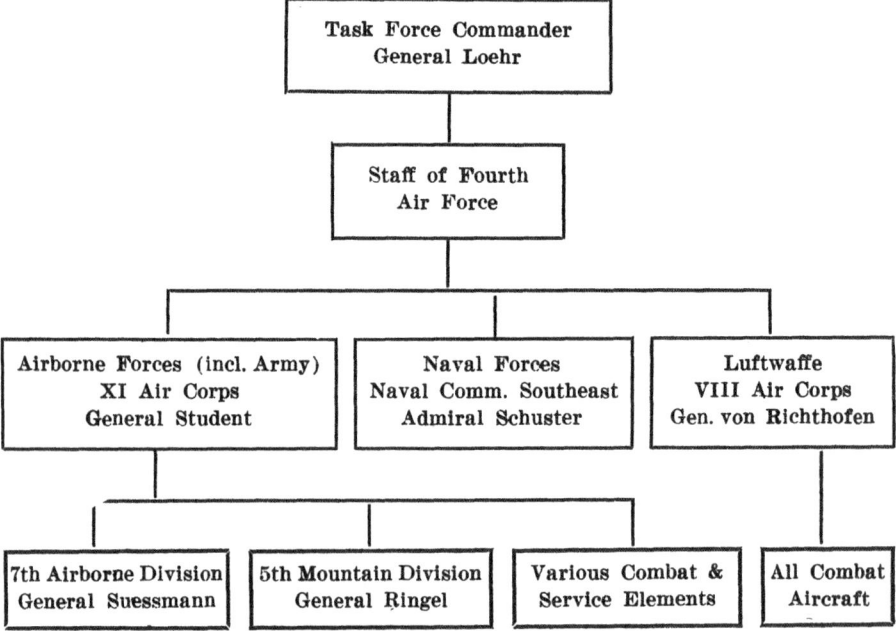

In contrast to the simplicity of this command organization, the British ground and air force units were under independent local commanders who in turn were subordinate to the respective service commanders, Middle East, stationed in Egypt. The naval commander sailed with the fleet. All three service commanders, Middle East, reported through their ministries to the War Cabinet in London and received their orders from that source. To add to the confusion, General Freyberg, the New Zealand commander of the ground forces, also reported to his government half way around the world whenever he felt that this was necessary or in the interest of his country.*

Prime Minister Churchill sent messages directly to General Freyberg and intervened when he believed that his influence and encouragement would be of benefit. Thus, on 27 May, at a time when the fate of Crete was no longer in doubt and the local commander was preparing orders for withdrawal, Churchill telegraphed to the commanders-in-chief, Middle East: "Victory in Crete essential at this turning-point in the war. Keep hurling in all you can."**

d. The element of surprise is essential to the success of an airborne operation which involves great risks under any circumstances. To achieve surprise, it is particularly important to maintain the secrecy of the offensive plans until the last minute. This will never be fully accomplished but several measures may be taken to deceive the enemy at least with regard to the exact time for the start of the attack. For example, whereas the logistical preparations at the jumpoff airfields for troop carriers and gliders may be accomplished well ahead of time, the airborne formations proper should be moved in as late as possible. The presence of parachute troops should be kept secret by restricting movements to and from the airfields of departure. Also, the enemy must be prevented from flying reconnaissance missions over the staging areas.

e. Other important factors are the intensive collection of intelligence and proper dissemination of information obtained. The terrain of the potential landing areas must be thoroughly reconnoitered by low-flying planes, aerial photography, and agents. By the time the parachute troops descend, the main enemy nests of resistance and defensive weapons must have been neutralized or the rate of jump casualties will be abnormally high.

German air reconnaissance during the period preceding the invasion was inadequate and the intelligence picture presented by the Luftwaffe did not correspond to the actual situation on the island. The British had succeeded in concealing fortifications and camouflaging their gun positions. Dummy flak positions were extensively bombed, while the real ones were not discovered. Some British positions were erroneously marked as artesian wells and the prison on the road to Canea was thought to be a British ration dump. Apparently, Twelfth Army had

---
*Winston S. Churchill, *The Grand Alliance*, pp. 274–75.
**Ibid., p. 295.

Figure 40. Airborne landings over the north coast of Crete.

more accurate information from local agents. But, in the firm belief that the British intended to evacuate the island immediately after the first airborne landings and that the garrisons consisted of only 5,000 combat troops, the Luftwaffe refused to consider more realistic estimates of the enemy preparations.

f. Airborne tactics must be flexible. After the seizure of Crete the Germans learned from captured documents that the British had studied the German operation orders pertaining to the airborne invasion of Holland in 1940 and had used the information for troop training purposes and for the construction of fortifications. Since the Germans had not changed their tactics, the enemy defense system proved entirely adequate during the first stage of the invasion. Had the Luftwaffe adopted different tactics, such as limiting the number of initial objectives to one or two, it could have achieved a greater concentration of forces. Moreover, the first waves of parachute troops jumped over the three airfields and landed amidst the concentrated fire of all defensive weapons the enemy had emplaced near each one of them. The purpose of landing on top of the objective, instead of near it, was to immediately paralyze the principal defense centers. This plan failed in each instance and its execution involved heavy casualties.

To make matters worse the troops jumped at the wrong points in most instances. Some units were dropped ten miles too far east. This was all the less comprehensible because the drop points had been clearly identified and the flying crews thoroughly briefed. Some of the pilots dropped the paratroopers in the wrong place and from too high an altitude so as to escape the enemy's ground fire. Their conduct jeopardized the success of the operation.

In any event a strong and well-integrated defense system cannot be overcome by landing on top of it, unless it has previously been smashed by continuous bombing attacks. Far better results can be obtained by jumping at a distance from the objective, which must subsequently be reduced by customary infantry tactics. For this purpose the paratrooper must receive infantry training.

g. Strong reserves, including flying formations, must be readily available so that any initial success, achieved wherever airborne landings have taken place, can be immediately exploited. Or, if unexpected difficulties arise, as in the Crete operation where the British fleet suddenly intervened, these reserves must be capable of immediate effective counteraction.

Figure 41. Antitank gun, attached to five parachutes, is dropped over Crete.

h. Individual soldiers must carry light machine guns, recoilless rifles, rocket launchers, etc., during the descent in case they are forced to fight before recovering their paracrates. The containers dropped by the Germans often fell into the enemy positions and were picked up by British troops who used the weapons and ammunition against the Germans, inflicting heavy causalties on them with their own weapons. Moreover, some of the containers fell into gullies and deep stream beds and could therefore not be recovered.

i. The troops must be issued appropriate uniforms. The German paratroop uniform proved unsuitable for the hot climate of Crete. During combat many men suffered from heat prostration. Every movement on the battlefield involved terrific physical efforts, and the efficiency of the troops was thus considerably impaired.

In evaluating the defender's performance General Ringel, who was in comand of German ground operations during the crucial battle for Canea, made the following statement: "The enemy's stubborn defense could have led to our defeat, if he had grasped the situation from the very outset and had made use of all his available forces and resources."

Chapter 23
Conclusions

Because of its daring execution and the novel techniques employed, the airborne invasion of Crete may be considered an historic military achievement. However, its many deficiencies, most of which are to be attributed to insufficient preparations, gave the operation all the characteristics of an improvisation. Despite the success achieved, the high cost of the seizure of the island led Hitler to lose confidence in airborne operations.

The possession of Crete proved of little offensive value to the Axis Powers because subsequent developments in the overall situation prevented them from exploiting their success. To the Germans Crete was not a stepping-stone to Suez and the Middle East, but rather the concluding part of the campaign in the Balkans.

One of the first effects of the Russian campaign, which started only twenty-one days after the cessation of hostilities in Crete, was the withdrawal of German air power from the eastern Mediterranean. Moreover, after October 1941 the shortage of trained ground forces compelled the German command to commit trained airborne and parachute units as infantry in Russia. General Student therefore seems to have been justified in stating in a post-war interrogation that "Crete was the grave of the German parachutists."

PART FIVE
THE RELATIONSHIP BETWEEN THE CAMPAIGNS IN THE BALKANS AND THE INVASION OF RUSSIA

By its intervention in the Balkans in 1940-41 Britain actually opened a second front several months before the first front—in Russia—had come into being. That this strategic move was largely abortive and had little immediate effect on the execution of Operation BARBAROSSA seems only incidental. The Axis Powers enlarged their area of responsibility by occupying territories whose economic potential was of some importance, but whose strategic advantages they were unable to exploit. Resenting occupation by Italian forces, Greek and Yugoslav nationalists were soon to rise against their conquerors. From that time through the end of World War II, the the Balkan sore in the Axis flank refused to heal.

Actually, Germany had little choice in the matter of launching the campaigns in the Balkans. Once Mussolini had committed the blunder of thrusting his blunt sword across the Albanian border into Greece and had suffered bitter reverses, Hitler felt obliged to rescue his brother-in-arms. Aside from reasons of prestige, Hitler's hand was forced by the British occupation of Crete and other Greek islands as well as by subsequent Russian and British political activities in the Balkans. The threat to Germany's southern flank in the impending invasion of Russia could either be eliminated by a lightning offensive or neutralized by creating a defensive belt of security in the Balkans. The former solution, which Hitler decided to adopt, had the advantage that only relatively small forces were tied down. Had the Germans adopted defensive methods, they would probably have had to commit more forces in the Balkans in the long run. A minimum force of three divisions would inevitably have been needed in Albania to support the Italians. Sooner or later the British would have succeeded in drawing Yugoslavia into the war on their side. If this had happened while Germany was engaged in hostilities with the USSR, an extremely dangerous situation might have developed.

Assuming therefore that the Germans were forced to execute the Balkan campaigns before they invaded Russia, the next step is to analyze the connection between these military operations.

Chapter 24

Influence of the Plans for Operation BARBAROSSA on the Campaigns in the Balkans

I. Hasty Execution of the Balkan Campaigns

In order to avoid any unnecessary delay in launching Operation BARBAROSSA, the two campaigns in the Balkans and the seizure of Crete had to be carried out with utmost speed. In many instances during the Yugoslav campaign divisions could not be fully assembled, and advance echelons had to jump off while the rear elements were still on the move to the concentration areas. The haste with which Crete had to be seized led to a number of improvisations in the preparation and execution of this airborne operation. Many of the deficiencies could have been avoided, had the Germans not been so pressed for time.

II. Hurried Redeployment from the Balkans

Even before the German victories in Yugoslavia and Greece had been fully achieved, some of the units had to be redeployed to Germany to be refitted in time for Operation BARBAROSSA. Some of the corps headquarters, GHQ units, and, above all, the mechanized divisions committed in the Yugoslav campaign were indispensable for the start of the invasion of Russia. In some instances units were stopped in mid-action and redeployed to the zone of interior. Because of the poor roads and defective railways in the Balkans, these movements interfered with the smooth execution of the military operations.

III. Defective Occupation of Yugoslavia and Greece

The insistence on speedy redeployment made it impossible to completely disarm the enemy forces or comb out the mountain areas in which some of the stragglers found refuge. Many weapons were hidden and stocks of military supplies vanished before they could be seized. The early rise of resistance and partisan movements in the Balkans was facilitated by the haste with which military operations in this theater had to be brought to an end.

Chapter 25
Effect of the Balkan Campaigns on Operation BARBAROSSA

I. Delay of Operation BARBAROSSA

Because of the annual spring floods in eastern Poland and western European Russia, 15 May was the earliest possible date for the start of the invasion of Russia. No postponement was mentioned before the Yugoslav revolt, which had an immediate effect on the plans for Operation BARBAROSSA. As early as 27 March Hitler estimated that the campaign against Yugoslavia would delay the invasion by about four weeks. This estimate was based on the diversion of forces for the assembly against Yugoslavia. Headquarters staffs, divisions, and GHQ units that were on the way to the concentration areas for Operation BARBAROSSA or whose departure was imminent had to be diverted. Those units had to be replaced by others whose departure was delayed because they were not ready for commitment. However, of the two corps headquarters and nine divisions that were diverted to the Yugoslav campaign, all but three infantry divisions were replaced from the Army High Command reserves by the time Operation BARBAROSSA got under way.

Another factor considered in calculating the delay was that all units, in particular the armored and motorized infantry divisions, would have to be refitted after the Balkan campaigns. This rehabilitation, which was estimated to take a minimum of three weeks for the mobile units, had to be performed within Germany in the vicinity of major repair shops and spare parts depots.

The plans for the invasion of Russia were modified in accordance with this estimate. On 7 April Field Marshal von Brauchitsch issued an order in which he explained that Operation 25 necessitated changes in the preparations for the Russian campaign postponing it between four and six weeks. The new target date was to be 22 June. Subsequent conferences between Hitler and his military advisers confirmed this new date for D-day, and it was adhered to in the end.

Actually, only part of the delay was caused by the campaigns in the Balkans. Operation BARBAROSSA could not possibly have started on 15 May because spring came late in 1941. As late as the beginning of June the Polish-Russian river valleys were still flooded and partly impassable as a result of exceptionally heavy rains.

II. The Redeployment of the Ground Forces

As soon as it became apparent that the Yugoslav campaign would be over within a relatively short time, the movement of forces destined for the Balkans was stopped and reversed. As early as 14 April three corps and seven divisions were rerouted to their respective points of departure in Germany and Romania. The redeployment of mobile divisions employed in Yugoslavia started on 21 April when the 16th Motorized Infantry Division was ordered to reassemble before entraining for Germany. Two days later three of the panzer divisions received similar orders.

While the campaigns in the Balkans were under way, the German Army hurriedly organized weak security divisions that were to be sent to western Europe and the Balkans for occupation duty. By the end of May five of these divisions had arrived in Yugoslavia and taken the place of all the combat divisions still remaining in that country. All but three of the German divisions employed in the Greek and Crete campaigns were redeployed before the beginning of Operation BARBAROSSA. Only the 2d and 5th Panzer Divisions, which had advanced as far as southern Greece, were not available in time for the start of the invasion.

III. The Influence on Air Operations

The considerable losses suffered by the Luftwaffe during the seizure of Crete, especially insofar as troop carrier planes were concerned, affected the strength of the German air power available at the start of the Russian campaign. Moreover, since the German parachute troops had been decimated in Crete, the number of men qualified to carry out large-scale airborne operations at the beginning of the invasion was insufficient.

As previously mentioned, the timetable for the attack on Russia did not allow for exploiting the strategic advantages the Germans had gained in the eastern Mediterranean. Even before the seizure of Crete had been accomplished, VIII Air Corps was ordered to redeploy its forces to Germany for refitting. While the ground personnel proceeded directly to their new bases in Poland, the flying units returned to Germany as soon as they could be released from participation in the Crete campaign. The movement along extended and complicated lines of communication had to be accomplished with maximum speed since it had to be completed in less than three weeks.

IV. The Balkan Campaigns as a Diversion

The German operations in the eastern Mediterranean in the spring of 1941 were successful in diverting world attention from the build-up in Poland. Coinciding with Rommel's advance in the North African desert, the German campaigns in the Balkans seemed to indicate that Hitler's plans of expansion were directed toward the eastern Mediterranean. The airborne seizure of Crete seemed to confirm the opinion that Hitler was bent on taking Suez by a combined air, sea, and ground operation. While the Russians were far from pleased to see the Balkans under German domination, they must have followed the diversion of German strength with great interest. The complete surprise achieved by the German invasion of Russia on 22 June may be partly attributed to the fact that the Balkan operations drew attention from the preparations that took place in Poland during April and May 1941.

Chapter 26

Conclusions

To form an unbiased opinion of the true relationship between the campaigns in the Balkans and the invasion of Russia is far from easy. German military authors state that the diversion in the Balkans had hardly any influence on the course of the subsequent campaign, since Germany's casualties were relatively low and the expenditure of materiel and supplies insignificant. They agree that the invasion of Russia might have started three weeks earlier if there had been no Balkan campaigns. This delay of three weeks might appear of decisive importance considering that the sudden start of severe winter weather turned the tide when the Germans stood in front of Moscow. To them the validity of this theory seems at least doubtful considering the fact that the German offensive in Russia in 1941 collapsed because of the conflict over the strategic concepts that broke out between Hitler and the Army High Command in the summer of that year. That controversy over the strategy to be adopted after the initial successes had been achieved cost the German Army several precious weeks. Additional time and a lot of manpower were wasted by Hitler's insistence on making Leningrad and the Ukraine his principal objectives until he finally agreed to a drive on Moscow before the outbreak of winter. The three weeks lost by the execution of the Balkan operations therefore seem of minor significance.

On the other hand, postwar publications by authors of other nationalities stress that the British intervention in Greece and Crete, and even more the Yugoslav revolt, led to the postponement of Operation BARBAROSSA to 22 June, while they deemphasize the effect of the spring floods.

In the light of the gigantic struggle that was to begin a few weeks after their conclusion, the campaigns in the Balkans may be considered as the Wehrmacht's last blitz victories before the Germans met their fate in Russia.

APPENDIX I

German Chain of Command at the Start of the Balkan Campaigns (6 April 1941)

- **Adolf Hitler** — CinC: Armed Forces
  - **Navy High Command** — CinC: Raeder
    - Naval Commander Southeast: Schuster
  - **Luftwaffe High Command** — CinC: Goering
    - Fourth Air Force — Comm. Gen.: Loehr
      - VIII Air Corps — Comm. Gen.: von Richthofen
  - **Army High Command (OKH)** — CinC: von Brauchitsch; Chief of General Staff: Halder; Dep. Chief of Staff: Paulus
  - **Armed Forces High Command (OKW)** — Chief of OKW: Keitel
    - Armed Forces Operations Staff — Chief: Jodl

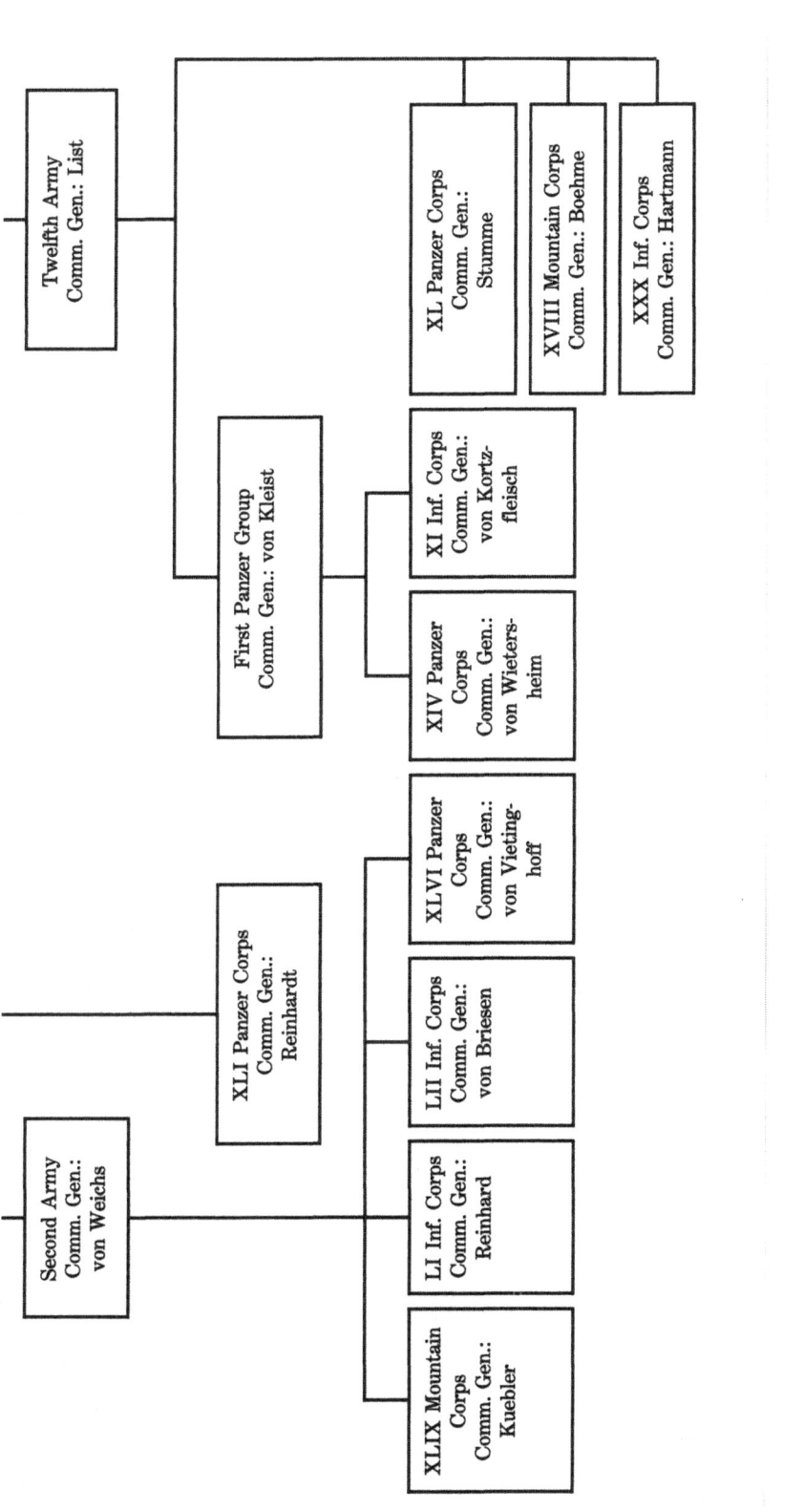

APPENDIX II

Chronological Table of Events

1940

May 1940
- 10 — Germany launches invasion of western Europe.

June 1940
- 10 — Italy declares war on Great Britain and France.
- 17 — Pro-Russian government established in Lithuania.
- 20 — Latvia and Estonia occupied by Russians.
- 22 — Franco-German armistice signed at Compiègne.
- 26 — Russia occupies Bessarabia and northern Bukovina.

July 1940
- 13 — Hitler discusses reason for continuance of British resistance at daily situation conference.
- 21 — During a staff meeting, Hitler first mentions possibility of a campaign against Russia.
- 31 — Hitler orders preparations for a campaign against Russia in spring of 1941.

August 1940
- 21 — Romania cedes the southern Dobrudja to Bulgaria.
- 30 — Vienna Arbitration Award: Romania yields one third of Transylvania to Hungary.

September 1940
- 13 — Italy begins drive into Egypt.
- 27 — Germany, Italy, and Japan sign the Tripartite Pact.

October 1940
- 7 — German troops enter Romania.
- 12 — Hitler postpones invasion of Great Britain until spring 1941.
- 28 — Italy invades Greece from Albania.
- 31 — British occupy Crete and Limnos.

November 1940
- 4 — Hitler orders preparations for eventual intervention in Greece.
- 4 — Royal Air Force begins to operate from Greek airfields.
- 12 — Directive No. 18 issued, enumerating the following objectives: capture of Gibraltar via Spain, seizure of Egypt and Suez Canal from Libyan bases, and invasion of Greece from Bulgaria.

November 1940

12–13	Molotov visits Berlin and confers with Hitler on future relationship between Germany and Soviet Union.
18	Hitler confers with King Boris of Bulgaria.
20	Hungary adheres to Tripartite Pact.
23	Romania joins Tripartite Pact.
28	Hitler confers with Yugoslav Foreign Minister Cincar-Marcovic and asks Yugoslavia to join Tripartite Pact.

December 1940

5	Hitler conference, Army plans for campaigns against Greece and Russia presented.
9	British start counterattack in North Africa and advance across Libya.
11	Hitler abandons plan to capture Gibraltar.
13	Directive No. 20 is issued, outlining Operation MARITA, the campaign against Greece.
18	Directive No. 21 issued, ordering preparations for Operation BARBAROSSA, the campaign against Russia.

1941

January 1941

13	British offer to send ground forces is rejected by Greece.
18–20	Hitler meets Mussolini and informs him about intended German attack on Greece.

February 1941

14	Hitler urges Yugoslav Premier Cvetkovic to join Tripartite Pact.
17	Bulgaria and Turkey conclude treaty of friendship.
28	German troops bridge the Danube.
28	At a conference in Ankara, British Foreign Secretary Eden and President Inoenue of Turkey stress mutual respect and adherence to Turkish-British alliance, but Turkey refuses to intervene in Balkans.

March 1941

1	Bulgaria joins Tripartite Pact.
2	German troops enter Bulgaria.
4	Hitler sends message to President Inoenue of Turkey.
4	Hitler confers with Prince Regent Paul of Yugoslavia.
7	British Expeditionary Force begins to land in Greece.

March 1941
- 9–16   Italian spring offensive in Albania.
- 18   Yugoslav privy council decides to join Tripartite Pact.
- 24   Rommel starts drive through weak British defenses in North Africa.
- 25   Yugoslavia signs Tripartite Pact.
- 26–27   Yugoslav *coup d'état*.
- 27   General Simovic assumes power in Yugoslavia.
- 27   Directive No. 25 is issued, outlining Operation 25, the campaign against Yugoslavia.
- 29   Conference of German Army commanders responsible for campaign in Balkans.

April 1941
- 3   Croat leaders join Simovic government.
- 5   Soviet Union signs treaty of friendship and non-aggression with Yugoslavia.
- 6   German air bombardment of Belgrade.
- 6   Twelfth Army invades southern Yugoslavia and Greece.
- 6   Second Army launches limited-objective attacks against Yugoslavia.
- 7   Operation BARBAROSSA postponed to 22 June.
- 7   German troops enter Skoplje.
- 7   Metaxas Line pierced by German mountain troops.
- 8   First Panzer Group starts drive toward Belgrade.
- 9   2d Panzer Division elements capture Salonika; Greek Second Army capitulates.
- 9–10   XLVI Panzer Corps enters the race for Belgrade.
- 10   Start of Second Army drive on Zagreb and capture of the city.
- 10   Croatia proclaims itself an independent state.
- 10   XLIX Mountain and LI Infantry Corps cross northwestern Yugoslav border.
- 10   First Panzer Group reaches point forty miles from Yugoslav capital.
- 11   XLI Panzer Corps advances to within forty-five miles of Belgrade.
- 11   German mountain troops cross the Vardar.
- 12   Fall of Belgrade.
- 13   Greek First Army begins to withdraw from Albania.
- 14   XVIII Mountain Corps pierces Mount Olympus defenses.

April 1941

14	Beginning of Yugoslav armistice negotiations.
15	German troops enter Sarajevo.
15	Seizure of Lamia.
15	General Student submits his plan for the seizure of Crete to Goering.
17	Capture of Thasos.
17	Yugoslav representatives sign unconditional surrender.
18	German armistice with Yugoslavia becomes effective at 1200.
19	5th Panzer Division enters Plain of Thessaly.
19	XVIII Mountain Corps captures Larisa.
20	Seizure of Samothraki.
21	Greek First Army offers to surrender to Germans.
21	British withdraw air force from Greece.
21	Redeployment of German troops from Balkans begins.
23	Greek First Army signs surrender agreement with Germans and Italians.
24	Last British stand at Thermopylae.
25	Directive No. 28 covering Operation MERKUR, the seizure of Crete, is issued.
25	Seizure of Limnos.
26	German parachute troops seize the Isthmus and town of Corinth.
27	Panzer elements enter Athens.
29	German forces reach south coast of the Peloponnesus.
30	Hostilities cease in Greece.

May 1941

15	Tentative date for beginning of Operation BARBAROSSA.
20	Beginning of airborne invasion of Crete.
21	German mountain troops begin to land at Maleme airfield.
21-22	British Navy intercepts German seaborne invasion force approaching Crete.
22	Air-sea battle in Crete waters.
22	German forces secure the Maleme airhead.
23	British planes return to Heraklion airfield.
26	Canea falls.
27	Capture of Heraklion airfield.
28	British begin to withdraw to south coast of Crete.

May 1941
- 28   Italian landings at Sitia Bay.
- 28–29   British garrison evacuates Retimo.
- 29   German troops establish contact with Retimo force.
- 30   Relief of Heraklion forces.

June 1941
- 1   German forces reach Sphakia and complete seizure of Crete.
- 22   D-day for German invasion of Russia.

APPENDIX III

Bibliographic List

I. Classified Sources

1. Postwar German Manuscripts Prepared for the Office of the Chief of Military History:

   MS #B-250, "Answers to Questions concerning Greece, Crete and Russia," by General Warlimont.

   MS #B-271, "Questions Asked General Guderian" and "Answers Given by General Guderian," by General Guderian.

   MS #B-334, "Balkan Campaign 1941," by General von Vietinghoff.

   MS #B-524, Supplements to the Study, "The Balkan Campaign" (The Invasion of Greece), by General von Greiffenberg.

   MS #B-525, Supplements to the Study, "The Balkan Campaign" (The Invasion of Yugoslavia), by General von Greiffenberg.

   MS #B-638, Seizure of the Isthmus of Corinth on 26 April 1941.

   MS #B-639, Commitment of Parachute Troops in Crete.

   MS #B-641, Crete, May 1941.

   MS #B-642, VIII Air Corps Operations During the Greek Campaign.

   MS #B-643, VIII Air Corps Signal Communications During the Greek Campaign.

   MS #B-645, Supply Problems in Greece.

   MS #B-646, The Conquest of Crete.

   MS #C-065e, "Italy, Winter 1940-41," by Helmuth Greiner.

   MS #C-065g, "Military Events in the Balkans, 1941," by Helmuth Greiner.

   MS #C-065i, "Operation BARBAROSSA," by Helmuth Greiner.

   MS #C-100, "The German Campaign in Greece and Crete, 1941," by Gen. Hermann Burkhart Mueller-Hillebrand.

   MS #C-101, "The Relationship between the German Campaign in the Balkans and the Invasion of Russia," by Gen. Mueller-Hillebrand.

   MS #P-030, "The German Campaign in the Balkans, 1941—A Model of Crisis Planning," by Gen. Mueller-Hillebrand.

   MS #P-030, "The Improvisation of an Operation—German Preparations for Operations Against Yugoslavia in 1941," by Gen. Mueller-Hillebrand.

2. German Documents.
   a. *OKW:*
   Uebernahme Kroatiens und des serbischen Gebietes durch Italiener u. Bulgaren, Abt. Landesverteidigung, OKW/122.
   Weisungen Nr. 25, Yugoslavien, OKW/137.
   Akte MARITA Griechenland, 18.12.40–4.4.41, OKW/1608.
   Weisung Nr. 29, MERKUR, OKW/1813.
   Aegaeische Inseln, OKW/1815.
   Weisung 28, Transportation und Bereitstellung der Kraefte fuer Unternehmen MERKUR, OKW/1817.
   Weisung Nr. 22, Mithilfe deutscher Kraefte bei den Kaempfen im Mittelmeerraum, OKW/1821.
   Weisung Nr. 18, Verhaeltnis zu Frankreich, Spanien, Portugal, OKW/1828.
   "Die Operationen im Suedosten," by Oberstleutnant von Lossberg, OKW/Abt/L.

   b. *OKH* (Operations Division):
   Aufmarsch BARBAROSSA 1941, H–22/219.
   Aufmarschanweisungen BARBAROSSA, H–22/220.
   BARBAROSSA, Band 2, vom 29.4.41 bis 26.9.41, H–22/353.
   Schematische Kriegsgliederung, Op. Abt. III.

   c. *Army Group South*:
   Aufmarschanweisungen BARBAROSSA, H. Gr. Sued, Ia, Anlagen Nr. 1, 45 u. 76 z., Kriegstagebuch, Teil I, Gen. St. d.H. Op. Abt. 13–603,6.
   Heeresgruppe Sued Kriegstagebuch, I. Teil, 2.2.41–21.6.41, WB–1784 A.
   Kriegstagebuch der Heeresgruppe Sued, Abt. Ia, WB–1784 B.

   d. *Second Army*:
   Armee-Oberkommando 2, Kriegstagebuch 28.3.41–24.4.41, E 246/1.
   Armee-Oberkommando 2, Ia. Anlage zum Kriegstagebuch Yugoslavien. Erfahrungsberichte, 12.5–3.6.1941, E 187/7.
   Armee-Oberkommando 2. Anlage zum Kriegstagebuch Yugoslavien, Armeebefehle, 5.4–2.6.1941, E 187/8.
   Armee-Oberkommando 2, Waffenstillstandsverhandlungen, 14.4.41–16.4.41, E 188/3.
   2 AOK Handakte, Ia, Oberstlt. i.G. Feyerabend, E 252/2.
   Anlage zum Kriegstagebuch Yugoslavien, Gefechtsberichte, 5.4.41–20.6.41, Armee-Oberkommando 2, Ia, 16690/285.

Anlage zum Kriegstagebuch Yugoslavien, 5.4.41–20.6.1941. Armee-Oberkommando 2, Ia, 16690/286.

Armee-Oberkommando 2, Ia, Nr. 1008/41 geh., 16690/287.

Armeebefehle–Bespr. m.d. Kdr. Gen. Aufmarschanweisung Yugoslavien, Gliederung der 2. Armee, 4.4.41–11.5.41, Balkan.

e. Twelfth Army:

Der Balkanfeldzug der 12.Armee. Generalfeldmarschall List–Ein strategischer Ueberblick, written by Ernst Wisshaupt, E 60.3.

Balkanfeldzug der 12.Armee 1941–Bilderbericht, 15078/1.

f. Wartime Propaganda Books:

Bathe, Dr. Rolf, *Der Kampf um den Balkan,* Gerhard Stalling Verlagsbuchhandlung, Oldenburg/Berlin, 1942. (Lib 2748).

Von Serbien bis Kreta, Prepared by a German Armed Forces Propaganda Company. (Lib 100).

Vorstoss nach Bosnien, Prepared by LI Infantry Corps, 1941. (Lib 2746).

Gebirgsjaeger auf Kreta, Prepared by Major Flecker, Intelligence Officer of 5th Mountain Division, Wilhelm Limpert Verlag, Berlin, 1942. (Lib 2749).

Panzer am Balkan, Prepared by the Panzer Propaganda Company of Panzer Group Kleist, Wilhelm Limpert Verlag, Berlin, 1941. (Lib 2747).

Kreta, Sieg der Kuehnsten, Prepared by General Student, Steirische Verlagsanstalt, Graz, 1942. (Lib 2718).

Ramcke, Bernhard, *Vom Schiffsjungen zum Fallschirmjaegergeneral,* Verlag "Die Wehrmacht," 1943.

3. Various German Situation Maps.
4. U. S. Military Documents:

Ciano Papers (Rose Garden), 1940–43

Mussolini's Private Papers (1939–42)

Fuehrer Directives and other Top Level Directives of the German Armed Forces, 1939–41, ONI, Washington, D. C., 1948.

The Private War Journal of Generaloberst Franz Halder, Chief of the General Staff of OKH, 14 Aug. 1939–24 Sep. 1942. Volumes V, VI, and VIII.

Special Bulletin No. 35, MID, War Dept., Washington, D. C., Oct. 15, 1941. G–2/2657–231.

Air-Borne Invasion of Crete, MID, War Dept. Gen. Staff File: 4402–100.

Early Campaigns of World War II, Dept. of Military Art & Engineering, U. S. Military Academy, West Point, N. Y., 1951.

"Airborne Operations—A German Appraisal," CMH Pub 104-13, October 1951.

5. U. S. State Department Document:

Blackstock, Paul W., *Indications of Soviet Plans and Intentions in German-Soviet Relations*, Western European Branch, State Department.

6. British Military Documents:

Gaul, W., *The German Occupation of Crete (Operation MERKUR)*. (Restricted).

"The Rise and Fall of the German Air Force for 1933–45," issued by the British Air Ministry, 1948 (ACAS [I]).

II. Unclassified Sources

Assmann, Kurt, *Deutsche Schicksalsjahre*, Eberhard Brockhaus, Wiesbaden, 1950.

Bullock, Alan, *Hitler, A Study in Tyranny*, Harper & Brothers, New York, 1952.

Brassey's Naval Annual 1948, edited by Rear Admiral H. G. Thursfield, The Macmillan Company, New York, 1948.

Churchill, Winston S., *The Grand Alliance*, Houghton Mifflin Co., Boston, The Riverside Press, Cambridge, 1950.

de Guingand, Maj. General Sir Francis, *Operation Victory*, Charles Scribner's Sons, 1947.

Fotitch, Constantin, *The War We Lost—Yugoslavia's Tragedy and the Failure of the West*, The Viking Press, New York, 1948.

Miksche, Major F. O., *Paratroops*, Random House, New York, 1943.

Papagos, General Alexander, *The Battle of Greece 1940–1941*, The I. M. Scazikis "Alpha" Editions, Athens, 1949.

Seton-Watson, Hugh, *The East European Revolution*, Methuen & Co. Ltd., London, 1950.

Von Tippelskirch, Kurt, *Geschichte des Zweiten Weltkriegs*, Athenaeum Verlag, Bonn, 1951.

Wards, I. McL., *The Other Side of the Hill*, War History Branch, Department of Internal Affairs, Wellington, New Zealand, 1952.

www.ingramcontent.com/pod-product-compliance
Lightning Source LLC
Chambersburg PA
CBHW060525100426
42743CB00009B/1433